MyWW
Points Co

MW00915489

Eat Smarter and Improve Overall Health with Selected and Most Delicious Freestyle Smart points Recipes

By

Dr. Leonard Ortiz

Table of Contents

DAY 1

Break Fast
Homemade Onion Soup Mix

Prep Time: 5 mins
Points Values: 10

Ingredients:

- 3 t parsley & ¾ C onion chopped or minced
- 2 t onion powder, 1 t turmeric , ½ t kosher salt
- ½ t ground black pepper , ½ t celery seed

Instructions

- First stir ingredients to mix and store in airtight container.
- About 1/3 cup equals one packet of store bought onion soup mix.

Nutrition Facts Per Serving Calories: 78kcal , Carbohydrates: 17g ,Protein: 2g

Lunch
Cilantro Lime Chicken Drumsticks

Prep Time5 mins, Cook Time20 mins Servings: 3 s
Points Values: 6

Ingredients

- 6 drumsticks , 1 tbsp. olive oil , 4 cloves minced garlic
- 1 tsp. crushed red peppers , 1 tsp. cayenne pepper
- 1 tsp. salt , Juice from 1 lime
- 2 tbsp. chopped cilantro , 1/2 cup chicken broth

Instructions

- Now add the olive oil to the Instant Pot and turn to sautÈ. When the oil is hot add the drumsticks. Sprinkle the seasoning over the drumsticks. Use tongs to stir the drumsticks and brown on each side for 2 minutes.
- Then add the lime juice, cilantro, and chicken broth to the Instant Pot. Lock the lid into place and turn the pressure valve to sealing. Cook on high pressure for 9 minutes. When done let the pressure release naturally.
- Transfer the drumstick to a baking sheet and broil until golden brown for about 3-5 minutes. Sprinkle with more cilantro and serve while warm.

Nutrition Facts Per Serving Serving: 2drumsticks, Calories: 480kcal, Carbohydrates: 3.3g, Protein: 47.2g

Dinner
Weight Watchers Instant Pot Potato and Shrimp Soup

Prep Time15 mins //Cook Time20 mins Servings: 8
Points Values: 3.25

Ingredients

- 2 Tbsp. of butter , 1 Can of corn low sodium
- 1 Glove of garlic minced , 1 Medium yellow onion
- ¼ cup of flour, 2 cups of diced potatoes
- 5 Cup of Vegetable Broth or Chicken Broth Fat Free
- 1 Cup of 1% low-fat milk , 1 Bay leaf
- ½ tsp dried Thyme
- 16 oz Shrimp peeled and deveined thawed

Instructions

- First set the Instant Pot to Sauté and add the butter, garlic, onions and corn. Stir and cook until onions are cooked.
- Now it is time to add the broth and potatoes, thyme and bay leaf. Set Instant Pot to Manual for 15 minutes.
- Once it's done, add the milk, flour and stir. Add the shrimp and seal IP for a couple of minutes. You do not have to turn the IP back on. It is still hot and will cook the shrimp with the lid on. Let the shrimp fully cook before serving

Nutrition Facts Per Serving This has 8 servings that are one cup each. Each cup is about 3.25 Freestyle SmartPoints.

DAY 2

Break Fast
Weight Watchers Homemade Sausage

Prep Time10 mins //Cook Time5 mins Servings: 4
Points Values:13

Ingredients:

- 1 tsp. cinnamon & 1 pound ground turkey or chicken
- 1 tsp nutmeg , 1/2 tsp salt , 1/2 green apple chopped small
- 1/4 C bone broth , 2 T coconut oil if frying

Instructions

- Put meat, apple, broth, and spices into a mixing bowl.
- Mix the ingredients together with your hands. Form into 12 small patties.
- Heat coconut oil in large pan and add sausage patties to hot oil. Cook for about 5 minutes, flipping half way.
- You can also bake these in the oven - it's less messy!

Nutritional Facts Per Serving Calories: 206kcal, Carbohydrates: 4g, Protein: 27g , Fat: 9g , Saturated Fat: 6g //Cholesterol: 62mg

Lunch
Turkey Meatball Stroganoff

Prep+Cook time:40 minutes, Servings: 4, Smart Points : 7

Ingredients:

- 1/2 cup chopped onion & 1 teaspoon olive oil, divided
- 1 pound 93% ground turkey
- 1/3 cup whole wheat seasoned breadcrumbs
- 1 large egg, beaten & 1/4 cup chopped parsley, divided
- 3 tbsp fat free milk & 3/4 tsp kosher salt
- black pepper, to taste & 3/4 cups water
- 1/2 cup light sour cream & 2 tbsp all purpose flour
- 2 teaspoons tomato paste
- 2 teaspoons beef Bouillon (I like Better Than Bouillon)
- 1/2 teaspoon Worcestershire sauce & 1/2 teaspoon paprika
- 8 ounces sliced Cremini mushrooms & 1 sprig fresh thyme

Instructions:
- First heat a large nonstick skillet or set the Instant Pot to saute and spray with oil; saute the onions over medium heat until golden, stirring 2 to 3 minutes. Remove and divide in two.
- In a large bowl, combine half of the sautéed onions with the ground turkey, bread crumbs, egg, 2 tbsp of the parsley, milk, 3/4 tsp salt and black pepper. Gently shape into 20 meatballs. In a blender combine the water, sour cream, flour, tomato paste, boullion, Worcestershire sauce and paprika, blend until smooth.
- Heat the skillet or Instant Pot back on saute, add the oil and brown half of the meatballs without disturbing (in two batches) about 2 minutes until no longer sticks, turn and brown an additional 2 minutes, set aside on a dish

and repeat with remaining meatballs. Place all the meatballs and remaining onion into the Instant pot, Slow Cooker or a large saucepan and pour the sauce over the meatballs along with the thyme and mushrooms.

o   For the Instant Pot: cook on high pressure 10 minutes. Let the pressure release on it's own. When done, discard thyme, add the chopped parsley and serve over your favorite noodles.

o   For the stove top: add 2 tbsp water, bring to a boil then cook covered on low 20 to 25 minutes. When done, discard thyme, add the chopped parsley and serve over your favorite noodles.

o   For slow cooker: cook on low 6 to 8 hours. When done, discard thyme, add the chopped parsley and serve over your favorite noodles.

Nutrition info per serving : Calories: 310 calories, Total Fat: 16g ,Saturated Fat: g, Cholesterol: 142mg, Sodium: 372mg ,Carbohydrates: 14.5g, Fiber: 2g, Sugar: 2g, Protein: 27.5g

Dinner
Instant Pot Garlicky Cuban Pork

Total Time:80 minutes plus marinade time
Servings : 10, Serving Size: a little over 3 oz
Points Values:5

Ingredients:

o 3 lb boneless pork shoulder blade roast, lean, all fat removed
o 6 cloves garlic & juice of 1 grapefruit (about 2/3 cup)
o juice of 1 lime , 1/2 tablespoon fresh oregano
o 1/2 tablespoon cumin , 1 tablespoon kosher salt
o 1 bay leaf & lime wedges, for serving
o chopped cilantro, for serving & hot sauce, for serving
o tortillas, optional for serving & salsa, optional for serving

Instructions:

• Cut the pork in 4 pieces and place in a bowl. In a small blender or mini food processor, combine garlic, grapefruit juice, lime juice, oregano, cumin and salt and blend until smooth.
• Pour the marinade over the pork and let it sit room temperature 1 hour or refrigerated as long as overnight.
• Transfer to the pressure cooker, add the bay leaf, cover and cook high pressure 80 minutes. Let the pressure release naturally.
• Remove pork and shred using two forks. Remove liquid from pressure cooker, reserving then place the pork back into pressure cooker. Add about 1 cup of the liquid

(jus) back, adjust the salt as needed and keep warm until you're ready to eat.

Nutrition Facts Per Serving Calories: 213 calories / Total Fat: 9.5g / Saturated Fat: 0g / Cholesterol: 91mg

DAY 3

Break Fast
Starbucks Sous Vide Egg Bites (Instant Pot)

Prep Time 10 mins // Cook Time 18 mins Servings : 4
Points Values:5

Ingredients

- ⇨ 4 Large Eggs , 4 strips bacon (Pork or Turkey)
- ⇨ 3/4 cup Favorite Cheese , 1/2 cup Cottage Cheese
- ⇨ 1/4 cup Heavy Cream , 1/2 tsp Salt
- ⇨ Optional: Dash of Hot Sauce

Instructions

- Put 1 cup of water in the bottom of your Instant Pot followed by the trivet that came with your pot.
- Cook the bacon utilizing your favorite method to cook bacon. Crumble and evenly distribute into 4 mason jars.
- Add the eggs, cheese, cottage cheese, cream and salt to the blender and blend until smooth (about 15 seconds).
- Add a dash of hot sauce if desired and blend for a few more seconds.
- Spritz the mason jars with spray oil (no need if using silicon molds)

- Divvy the egg mixture evenly into 4 mason jars.
- Cover each mason jar loosely with foil and place gently in the Instant Pot.
- Place the cover on the Instant Pot and select "Steam" and set to 8 Minutes.
- NPR (natural pressure release) for 10 minutes and then quick release (QR) the rest.
- Carefully remove the egg bites from the Instant Pot and let cool down for a few minutes.
- Enjoy immediately or refrigerate for up to a week!

Nutrition Facts Per Serving 170 calories, 7g of fat, 13g of carbs

Lunch
Instant Pot Parmesan Garlic Artichokes
Prep+Cook time: 17 mins, SmartPoint : 1, Servings: 4

Ingredients

- 4 artichokes & 2 tsp minced garlic
- 4 tsp olive oil , 1/4 cup grated or shredded parmesan cheese
- 1/2 chicken or vegetable broth water also works

Instructions

- o Wash and trim artichokes, removing the top of the artichoke, outer leaves and stem.
- o Spread each artichoke open and top each one with 1/2 tsp minced garlic and drizzle 1 tsp of olive oil over top.
- o Sprinkle each artichoke with 1 tbsp grated or shredded parmesan cheese. Using basket insert, place artichokes in the Instant Pot. Pour in 1/2 cup of chicken or vegetable both. You can also use water.

o   Seal Instant Pot, making sure valve is set to seal. Select the steam option and cook for 10 minutes. NOTE: If you have smaller artichokes, you might want to reduce cooking time by a couple minutes. Once cooking is complete, quick release steam by moving valve to venting. Reminder to use an oven mit to protect hands from steam.

Nutrition info per serving : Calories 128 Calories from Fat 54, Total Fat 6g 9%, Saturated Fat 1g 5%, Cholesterol 5mg 2% , Sodium 216mg 9% , Potassium 473mg 14% , Total Carbohydrates 14g 5% , Dietary Fiber 6g 24% , Sugars 1g , Protein 6g 12%

Dinner
Instant Pot Shredded Mexican Chicken

Prep Time 5 mins // Cook Time15 mins Servings: 6
Points Values:4

Ingredients

o   2 lbs boneless, skinless chicken breasts frozen
o   1.2 c non-fat, low-sodium chicken broth
o   2 10-oz cans Rotel fire-roasted diced tomatoes and green chiles, undrained
o   2 15-oz cans black beans, rinsed and drained
o   3-4 garlic cloves, minced & 1 small jalapeno pepper, finely diced
o   1 T hickory-flavored liquid smoke (if you leave this out, you'll be fine) & 2 tsp ground cumin
o   1 T chili powder, 1 tsp smoked paprika
o   2 tsp dried oregano
o   1 tsp cayenne pepper (leave this out if it's too spicy)

- o salt and pepper to taste & 2 limes, quartered
- o 1.4 c fresh cilantro, chopped
- o Place the frozen chicken in your Instant Pot. Add all ingredients to the pot.

Instructions

- Lock the lid into place and make sure the pressure valve is set to seal. Set on manual for 16 minutes at high pressure. Let the pressure release naturally.
- Drain any liquid and shred the chicken. Serve with letuce wraps, plain, over rice or on corn tortillas.

Nutrition Facts Per Serving Calories 218 Calories from Fat 36 / Total Fat 4g / Saturated Fat 1g / Cholesterol 108mg / Sodium 437mg

DAY 4

Break Fast
Instant Pot Cinnamon Apples

Prep Time: 5 mins// Cook Time: 2 mins
Servings: 4-6, **Points Values:0**

Ingredients

o   3 apples (we like gala) , 1 heaping tsp cinnamon
o   1 heaping tsp maple syrup

Instructions

- Peel, core, and slice the apples. (I use this tool that does it all at once!).
- Combine apples, cinnamon, and maple syrup in the Instant Pot. Pour in 1/4 cup water. Stir quickly to coat the apples.
- Cook on high pressure for 2 minutes. Quick release. Serve immediately or remove lid and keep warm until you're ready (up to an hour).

Nutrition Facts Per Serving Serving Size: 4oz / Calories Per Serving: 42 / Cholesterol 0mg

Lunch
Instant Pot Chipotle Chicken Tacos

Prep Time: 15 mins//Cook Time: 20 mins Servings: 12
Points Values:3

Ingredients

o 1 medium onion chopped , 1 Tablespoon garlic minced
o 1 pound boneless chicken breasts , 1/2 cup chicken broth
o 2 Tablespoons chipotle chiles diced , 1 teaspoon brown sugar
o 1/2 teaspoon garlic powder
o 1 Tablespoon fresh cilantro chopped
o 1/2 small lime juiced , lettuce
o 1 medium tomato chopped , 12 6 inch tortillas
o 1/2 cup cheese shredded , olive oil spray

Instructions

• With the cooker's lid off, spray the olive oil spray and heat to "Saute" until the cooker has heated up. Add the onion and garlic and cook until the onion is translucent and the garlic is fragrant.
• Season the chicken breasts with salt and pepper and place in the Instant Pot and saute until browned. Add the chicken stock, chilies, brown sugar, cilantro and lime juice. Securely lock the pressure cooker's lid and set to "Manual". Cook at HIGH pressure for 8 minutes.

- Perform a quick release to release the pressure. Open the lid and remove the chicken breasts. Shred the chicken and set it back in the cooker.
- Scoop out 1/2 cup of the chicken mixture onto a tortilla. Add lettuce, tomato and cheese, if desired and serve immediately.

Nutrition Facts Per Serving Calories: 148kcal / Carbohydrates: 13.1g / Protein: 10.9g /Fat: 5.9g / Saturated Fat: 2.1g / Cholesterol: 29.3mg

Dinner
Instant Pot Chicken Curry Recipe with Potatoes
Prep Time 10 mins// Cook Time 25 mins
Serves 6, **Points Values:9**

Ingredients

- 2 tsp olive oil , 1/2 yellow onion, chopped
- 1/2 Gala apple, chopped , 2 tbsp minced ginger
- 4 garlic cloves, minced & 6 tbsp mild curry paste
- 2 tsp ground coriander & 2 tsp ground cumin
- 2 tsp garam masala & 2 lb. boneless, skinless chicken thighs
- 1 lb. Little Potato Company Creamer potatoes (halved or quartered)
- 1 1/2 cup diced tomatoes
- 3/4 cup chicken broth & 3/4 cuplite coconut milk
- 1/2 tsp salt & 1/2 tsp ground pepper

Instructions

- Set the Instant Pot to the saute setting. Add the olive oil and allow to heat for 1 minute. Add the onion, apple and

21

ginger, and cook, stirring occasionally, until softened, about 5 minutes. Stir in the garlic, curry paste, coriander, cumin and garam masala, and cook for 1 minute.

- Add the chicken thighs, potatoes, tomatoes, chicken broth, coconut milk, salt and pepper, and stir to combine.
- Put the lid on the Instant Pot, close the steam vent and set to HIGH pressure using the manual setting. Decrease the time to 10 minutes.
- Once the time is expired, wait for 5 minutes, then carefully use the quick release valve to release the steam. Shred the chicken with two forks. Season to taste. Serve.

Nutrition Facts Per Serving Serving Size 1 cup / Calories 349.8 cal / Calories from fat 144

DAY 5

Break Fast

Easy Braised Chicken Drumsticks in Tomatillo Sauce

Prep+Cook time:30 minutes/pressure cooker,
Smart Points: 3, Servings: 6

Ingredients:

- 6 chicken drumsticks, on the bone, skin removed (24 oz)
- 1 tbsp cider vinegar & 1 tsp kosher salt
- 1/8 tsp black pepper & 1 teaspoon dried oregano
- 1 teaspoon olive oil
- 1 1/2 cups jarred tomatillo sauce (I used Frontera)
- 1/4 cup chopped cilantro, divided
- 1 jalapeno, halved and seeded

Instructions:

- o Season chicken with vinegar, salt, pepper and oregano. Marinate a few hours if time permits.
- o Set the Instant Pot to saute, when hot add the oil and the chicken to brown on both sides, about 4 minutes on each side.
- o Add the tomatillo salsa, 2 tablespoons of the cilantro and jalapeno, cover and cook on high pressure 20 minutes, until the chicken is tender. When the pressure releases, garnish with cilantro and serve over rice if desired.

Nutrition info per serving : Calories: 161 calories , Total Fat: 5g, Saturated Fat: 1g , Cholesterol: 101mg , Sodium: 736mg , Carbohydrates: 5g , Fiber: 0g , Sugar: 2g , Protein: 22g

Lunch
Instant Pot Jalapeno Dip
Prep Time 5 mins //Cook Time 15 mins Servings : 24
Points Values: 1

Ingredients

- o 1 Package fat free cream cheese
- o 1 cup fat free shredded cheddar cheese
- o 1/2 cup fat free sour cream
- o ½ cup shredded/diced chicken & ¼ cup diced jalapenos
- o ¼ cup diced green onions & ½ tsp cumin

For garnish:
- o A few sliced jalapenos
- o Sprinkle of pepper & Sprinkle of bread crumbs

Instructions

- Combine cream cheese, cheddar cheese, chicken, diced jalapenos, green onions, cumin, and pepper in the basin of your Instant Pot.
- Seal, set time to 5 minutes, and cook on "manual".
- Vent your cooker, open the lid, and stir in your sour cream until evenly blended.
- Pour into a serving dish and top with extra cheese, jalapenos, and bread crumbs.

Nutrition Facts Per Serving Per Serving: 80 calories; 6.6 g fat; 0.7 g carbohydrates; 4.7 g protein; 24 mg cholesterol; 137 mg sodium

Dinner
Weight Watchers Beef Gyros In The Instant Pot

Prep+Cook time: 25 mins, Servings: 6 , 8 Smart Points

Ingredients

- 2 lbs beef roast thinly sliced I've also used loin flap meat and it's so easy to slice and cook!
- 3 cloves minced garlic & 1 tbsp dried parsley
- 1 tsp black pepper , 1 tsp salt
- 1/2 cup vegetable broth , 1 red onion thinly sliced
- 1 tbsp lemon juice & 4 tbsp oil olive, coconut, avocado, etc
- 1 tsp apple cider vinegar optional , 1 tsp olive oil optional

Toppings

- Pitas or Naan bread or Flat Out pitas I love the Flat Out pitas the best!
- Sliced carrots , Sliced onions , Sliced cucumbers , Lettuce
- Feta or goat cheese optional, use container to measure

Tzatziki Sauce:
- 2 tbsp fresh dill & 1 cup plain Greek yogurt
- 1/2 cup cucumber peeled seeded and chopped
- 1 clove minced garlic , 1 tsp salt and pepper

Instructions

- o Turn Instant Pot on saute and let the pan warn up. When it's warm, add oil to the bottom of the pan and let it get hot.
- o Add meat, seasoning, garlic, and onion to Instant Pot. Sear and let onions soften for 3-5 minutes
- o Pour lemon juice and broth over the meat. Give the meat a quick stir, then lock lid into place. Turn the steam valve to sealing. Using the Meat/Stew preset cook the gyro meat for 9 minutes. Let the pressure naturally release for 3 minutes before releasing the remaining pressure using the quick release method.
- o While the gyro meat is cooking mix together the Tzatziki sauce and slice your vegetable toppings. For added flavor drizzle apple cider vinegar and olive oil over vegetables.
- o To make your gyro layer the lettuce at the bottom of the pita or naan bread. Then add your meat, toppings, and sauce. This will keep the pita or naan from getting soggy.

Nutrition info per serving : Calories: 535kcal, Carbohydrates: 27.1g, Protein: 54.5g, Fat: 22.7g, Saturated Fat: 6.1g

DAY 6

Break Fast
Tuscan Chicken Stew

Prep: 15 minutes , Cook: 35 minutes Servings: 6
Points Values:5

Ingredients:

- 1 1/2 lb. raw boneless skinless chicken breast
- 1/4 tsp. each salt and black pepper
- 4 cups roughly chopped kale
- Two 15-oz. cans cannellini (white kidney) beans, drained and rinsed
- 2 cups chopped tomatoes , 1 cup chopped onion
- 1 cup chicken broth , 1 1/2 tsp. chopped garlic
- 1 tsp. Italian seasoning , 1/2 tsp. onion powder

Instructions:

- Place chicken in the Instant Pot, and sprinkle with salt and pepper.
- Add remaining ingredients. Top with lid, aligning the lid arrow with the arrow marked Open. Rotate until aligned with the Close arrow. Set the pressure release valve to the Sealing position.
- Press the Manual button, and set time for 8 minutes. (The Instant Pot will preheat for 20 - 25 minutes.)
- Press the Keep Warm/Cancel button to turn off the Instant Pot.
- Caution: During the next step, keep hands and face away from opening; the fast-escaping steam will be hot! Turn the pressure release handle to the Venting position to let out steam until the float valve drops down.

- Transfer chicken to a large bowl. Shred with two forks.
- Return chicken to the pot, and stir.

Nutrition Facts Per Serving 1/6th of recipe (about 1 1/3 cups): 289 calories, 3.5g total fat (0.5g sat fat), 506mg sodium, 27.5g carbs, 8g fiber, 4.5g sugars, 35g protein

Lunch
Instant Pot Roasted Chicken Breast & Vegetables

Prep+Cook time: 35 mins , Serves: 4, SmartPoints: 3

Ingredients

- ½ Chicken or 2 Bone-In Chicken Breasts, 2 Cups Carrots
- 8 medium new potatoes (red or yellow)
- 1 cup pearl onions (or 1 onion chopped)
- ½ Cup Chicken Broth , 1 Spring Rosemary
- 1 Spring Thyme & 2 cloves garlic, minced
- 1 teaspoon salt , 1 teaspoon black pepper

Instructions

o Season chicken breasts with salt and pepper
o Spread olive oil over the bottom of Instant Pot and pour chicken broth into bottom of Instant Pot
o Place chicken on top of the broth and cover with onions, thyme, rosemary, and garlic. Top with carrots and potatoes (you may wish to season with salt and pepper)
o Place Instant Pot lid on and set to seal. Set to the Manual Setting for 20 minutes.
o Allow to NPR. Remove from Instant Pot.
o For those who want crispy skin, remove the chicken from the Instant Pot and place under the broiler for 5 minutes.

Dinner
Weight Watchers BBQ Pulled Pork Recipe

Cook Time15 mins Servings: 4, **Points Values:7**

Ingredients

- 1/2 cup Sugar Free BBQ sauce of choice
- 1 pound of uncooked lean pork tenderloin sliced
- 2 cups packaged coleslaw mix , 2 Tbsp light mayo
- 1 tsp apple cider vinegar
- 1/4 tsp stevia or less just for sweetness and taste
- 4 whole wheat bread thins

Instructions

- Cut and cube the pork tenderloin, then place in the crock pot on low for about 4 hours. Then remain on warm until you are ready to eat your meal. The internal temp needed for pork is 145 degrees Fahrenheit.
- Add BBQ sauce to meat in crock pot when you start cooking.
- Mix coleslaw with mayo, apple cider vinegar and stevia in a bowl. Set aside. Once meat is cooked and before serving, simply shred meat in the crock pot with a fork.
- Place 3 oz of BBQ pulled pork with 1/3 cup of slaw mix on your whole wheat bread thins and you are good to go!

Nutrition Facts Per Serving Calories 286 Calories from Fat 45 / Total Fat 5g 8% // Saturated Fat 1g 5% // Cholesterol 74mg 25% //Sodium 606mg 25% //Potassium 788mg 23% //Sugars 13g //Protein 29g

DAY 7

Break Fast
Banana oatmeal jam muffins

Prep+Cook time: 32 mins, Serves: 12, Smart points : 2

Ingredients

- 1 egg , 2 medium mashed bananas
- ⅓ cup milk (I used skim milk) , 1 tsp vanilla
- 1 tsp baking powder , ½ tsp cinnamon
- 2¼ cup oats (I used Quaker large flake oats, not a quick oat)
- No sugar added jam (I used Smucker's, apricot & raspberry)

Instructions
- o Preheat oven to 350F, spray a 12 hole regular muffin tin with some non stick spray.
- o In a bowl whisk together your milk & egg, add in mashed banana and vanilla. Stir in oats, baking powder and cinnamon.
- o Divide batter over your 12 muffin cups, make indents in the middle of your muffins to add the jam, drop by spoon, about ½-1 Tbsp in each. Bake in oven for 22 minutes and enjoy!

Nutrition info per serving : Calories 99, Fat 1.6g, Sat fat 0.4g, Carbs 18.7g,Fiber 2.7g, Sugars 4.7g, Protein 3.3g

Lunch
Campfire Stew

Prep Time 10 mins , Cook Time 50 mins , **Points Values: 5**

Ingredients

- o 1 onion chopped finely , 1 tbsp olive oil
- o 1.4 kg pork shoulder no bone all visible fat removed
- o 2 peppers bell deseeded and finely chopped
- o 2 garlic cloves minced
- o 2 tin black-eyed beans drained (or any beans you prefer)
- o 1 tin chopped tomatoes , 2 tbsp tomato puree
- o 2 tsp smoked paprika , 2 tsp caraway seeds
- o 2 tsp dried mixed herbs (Herbes de Provence)
- o 100 ml water or stock , Salt , Black pepper

Instructions

- (Optional step) Press 'Sauté' on the Instant Pot. Add oil and when hot, fry the onions for 5 mins. (Optional step) Then add in the boneless pork shoulder and brown on all sides.
- Place (the rest of – if you did the optional steps) the ingredients into the Instant Pot bowl, mix well and cover. Turn the vent to 'Sealing,' then set the pressure cooker to 'Manual' for 50 mins.
- When done let the vent naturally release. Transfer the pork to a plate and shred. (If the pork does not shred easily, add the joint back into the Instant Pot and cook for an additional 10 mins on high pressure.)

- (Optional step) Press the 'Sauté' button once more, and let the sauce simmer for 10-15 mins or until it has thickened and reduced by more than half.
- Return the shredded pork to the Instant Pot, stir and serve.

Nutrition Facts Per Serving Calories 358 Calories from Fat 108 /Total Fat 12g / Saturated Fat 3g /Cholesterol 147mg

Dinner
Instant Pot Brussels Sprouts with Bacon and Garlic

Prep+Cook time: 20 minutes, Servings : 4, SmartPoint : 1
Ingredients

- 3 cloves garlic minced , 3 shallots diced fine
- 1 pound fresh Brussels Sprouts
- 4 slices center cut bacon cut into 1/2" pieces
- 1/2 cup water

Instructions

- o Prepare Brussels sprouts by removing stems and halving larger pieces so they become bite-sized.
- o Mince garlic cloves, slice shallots and cut bacon into small pieces.
- o Turn Instant Pot to Saute, and add bacon to Instant Pot liner. Cook for 5-7 minutes or until it begins to render and crisp.
- o Add the remaining ingredients and stir well. Place lid on Instant Pot and set to seal.
- o Cook on manual high pressure for 4 minutes. Quick release and serve.

Nutrition info per serving : Makes 4 Servings , 1 SmartPoint pererving on Beyond the Scale, FreeStyle, and FlexPlan

DAY 8

Break Fast

FroYo Bark – Weight Watchers Freestyle

Prep Time 10 mins, Freeze time 1 hr, **Points Values:0**

Ingredients

- o 1 cup non-fat plain Greek yogurt
- o 1 teaspoon vanilla extract , 2 packets Splenda
- o 4-6 strawberries , 1 teaspoon cocoa powder (optional)

Instructions

- In a small bowl, mix the yogurt, vanilla and Splenda.
- Line an 8 x 8 baking pan with parchment paper. Pour the yogurt mixture into the pan evenly.
- Cut up the strawberries and add them to the yogurt. I pushed them into the yogurt slightly.
- Add the cocoa powder using a mesh strainer. Now Freeze for 2 hours.

Nutrition Facts Per Serving 8 Calories / 0 Fat / 1 Carb

Lunch
Best Pot Roast Recipe for Instant Pot

Prep+Cook time: 1 hour 25 mins, Serves: 8, Smart Points : 7

Ingredients

- 3 pound chuck roast, trimmed
- 2 teaspoons garlic powder , 2 teaspoons onion powder
- 1 teaspoon seasoned salt , 1 teaspoon black pepper
- 3 cloves garlic minced & 1 onion chopped
- 2 cups baby carrots & 8 small potatoes (new potatoes)
- ½ cup red wine & ½ cup beef broth

Instructions

- o In a small bowl, mix together the garlic powder, onion powder, seasoned salt, and black pepper.
- o Liberally sprinkle all sides of the roast with the seasoning blend.
- o Place roast in bottom of Instant Pot liner. Add in minced garlic.
- o Pour in the red wine and beef broth. Top with chopped onion and red pepper. Add carrots and potatoes on top of onion.
- o Place lid and set to seal. Choose Meat and set to 55 minutes. Allow to cook, and NPR (natural pressure release) for 15 minutes.
- o Remove from Instant Pot and shred to serve.

Dinner
Instant Pot Goulash

Prep Time5 mins, Cook Time10 mins Servings: 8
Points Values:3

Ingredients

- 1 lb ground turkey & 1 tbsp . minced garlic
- 2 1/2 tbsp Italian seasoning & 1 tbsp . minced onions
- 1 tsp . salt & 2 bay leaves & 1 chopped zucchini
- 1 cup chopped red and green bell peppers
- 8 oz . whole wheat pasta
- 1 - 14 oz can crushed tomatoes OR jarred sauce
- 1 can water (you'll be filling the tomato can with water)

Instructions

- Turn Instant Pot to saute and brown the ground turkey.
- Add your 1 tbsp. garlic, 1 tbsp. minced onions, 2 1/2 tbsp. Italian seasoning, 1 tsp. salt, and 2 bay leaves. Toss in your 1 chopped zucchini and 1 cup of red and green bell peppers.
- Mix so that the seasonings and veggies are distributed. Pour the 8 ounces of dry whole wheat pasta, can of crushed tomatoes (or a jar of pasta sauce), and fill the can back up with water and pour that over the vegetables.
- Stir until the pasta is fully mixed with the sauce. Lock the lid into place and turn the pressure valve to sealing. Cook on high pressure using the manual function for 10 minutes. Use the quick release method to release the pressure. Give it a stir and let the goulash cool for a few minutes–it's super hot!
- Top with cheese if desired and serve.

Nutrition Facts Per Serving Calories: 501kcal, Carbohydrates: 52.2g, Protein: 40.4g, Fat: 16.7g.

DAY 9

Break Fast
Instant Pot Eggs Benedict

Prep+Cook time: 14 minutes, Servings: 2, Smart Points: 5

Ingredients -In the Instant Pot:

- 1 cup of sliced cauliflower (so it'll fit underneath the trivet) (I weighed this and it was 3.2 oz, just fyi)
- 1 cup of water
- olive oil cooking spray , Egg mold (see below)
- 2 large eggs

Hollandaise:

- 1 egg yolk , 2 tsp lemon juice (or more to taste)
- 1/8 tsp salt , 1/8 tsp white pepper
- 1 Tbs unsalted butter, melted and hot
- All of the hot, cooked cauliflower from the Instant Pot, well drained

Benedict:

- 1 whole wheat English muffin, split and toasted
- 4 slices of low-sodium, fat-free ham
- chopped chives or green onions for garnish (optional)

Instructions

- o Spray two cups in your egg cup mold with the cooking spray and set aside.
- o Put your sliced cauliflower in the bottom (don't waste the cauliflower stem either, this is a perfect use for it!), cover with the water. Put your trivet on top, followed by your egg mold, cups, or ramekins. Crack an egg into a

small bowl (so you can make sure that you didn't break the yolk or get any shell in) and then carefully put it in the mold. Do the same with the second egg. Cover with your IP lid and set to manual for 2 minutes. I've found with my Instant Pot, manual for 2 minutes with a 3 minute NPR is the perfect cooking time, however, IPs vary and yours may require a little testing before you get this just right for you. I also noticed that when I didn't have the cauliflower in the bottom, it took 3 minutes on manual with a quick release. Your eggs should wiggle just slightly if you shake your pot. If they look watery, they're not done yet.

While your eggs are cooking:
- o In a small food processor or blender (I like using my ninja blender cup for this), put in the egg yolk, lemon juice, salt, and white pepper. Blend for 20 -30 seconds so it's ready to go when the Instant Pot is done.

When your eggs are done cooking:
- o Carefully remove your trivet from the pot, set aside.
- o Drain the cooked cauliflower and add it and the hot melted butter to your food processor or blender and process until smooth, thick and creamy.

Lunch
Buffalo Chicken Wings

Prep Time5 mins //Cook Time11 mins Servings: 4
Points Values: 3

Ingredients

o   2 lbs . 2 large breasts partially defrosted chicken breast cut into strips (I've also used frozen chicken breasts, please see below)
o   1/2 cup Franks Red Hot Sauce , 1 tsp . cayenne pepper
o   1 tsp . salt , 2 tbsp . butter , 1 tsp . pepper
o   1/4 cup Franks Red Hot Sauce for coating

Instructions

•   Turn the Instant Pot to saute to melt the butter. When it is melted add in the chicken, salt, pepper, and cayenne pepper. Mix the chicken so that each piece is seasoned.
•   I've also placed frozen chicken breasts in the Instant Pot, along with the other ingredients (minus butter), and cooked for 16 minutes. I cube the chicken after it's cooked and continue with the recipe.
•   Add 1/2 cup hot sauce then stir the chicken so that it is coated.
•   Lock the lid into place and turn the steam valve to sealing. Using the manual setting cook on high pressure for 8 minutes. If your chicken is fully defrosted cook for 7 minutes. I used partially defrosted chicken because it is easier to cut. Release the pressure using the quick release method.

- In a hurry? Drizzle warm sauce before serving and skip the last step!
- Using tongs, remove the chicken from the Instant Pot and place on a baking sheet lined with aluminum foil. Brush the chicken with the additional 1/4 cup hot sauce. Thicken the sauce by placing under the broiler for 3 minutes. Turn the chicken over and repeat on the other side. Let the chicken cool 5 minutes before serving. Goat cheese is tastes amazing spread on top.

Nutrition Facts Per Serving Weight Watchers, 1 Serving (Recipe Serves 4), 3 Freestyle Smart Points

Dinner
Instant Pot Mushroom Barley Soup

Prep+Cook time: 40 minutes, Servings 8, Smart Points : 2
Ingredients
- 8 cups beef or vegetable broth , 3/4 cup barley
- one medium onion chopped , 2 carrots chopped
- 4 cloves garlic minced , 1 lb sliced mushrooms
- 1 tsp salt , 1/2 tsp freshly ground pepper
- 1 Tbsp Steak Sauce

Instructions
- o Add all ingredients to the Instant Pot and stir well.
- o Set Instant Pot to Manual / High Pressure for 20 minutes.
- o Let pressure release naturally for 10 minutes then Quick Release
- o Stir well And Enjoy!

Nutrition info per serving : Amount Per Serving (1 g) , Calories 0

DAY 10

Break Fast

Instant Pot Italian Creamy Chicken Pasta Recipe

Prep time: 10 mins //Cook time: 15 mins Serves: 8
Points Values: 6

Makes 8 Servings 1½ cup per serving 8 SmartPoints per serving

Ingredients

- 1 pound boneless skinless chicken breast, cubed
- 16oz box penne pasta
- 2 cups chicken stock (or water)
- 2 Roma tomatoes, diced & ½ red onion, diced
- 1 cup mushrooms, diced
- 2 cloves garlic, minced (can use equivalent garlic powder if you prefer)
- 2 teaspoons Italian seasonings
- 1 cup low-fat part-skim mozzarella cheese, shredded
- ½ cup fat-free cream cheese

Instructions

- Add all ingredients to Instant Pot liner, except for cheeses.
- Mix well so that pasta is covered in liquid and everything is well combined.
- Place lid and set to seal.
- Set to high pressure (manual) for 9 minutes. Once done, allow to NPR (natural pressure release) for 5 minutes.

- Once pressure has released, remove the lid and stir in cheeses until well combined and melted.
- Serve with additional Parmesan or parsley as desired.

Nutritional Facts Makes 8 servings (1 1/2 cup per serving)

Lunch
Barbacoa Beef (Pressure Cooker or Instant Pot)

Prep/Cook time:1 hour 20 minutes, Smart Points : 3

Ingredients:

- 5 cloves garlic , 1/2 medium onion
- 1 lime, juice
- 2-4 tbsp chiptoles in adobo sauce(to taste)
- 1 tbsp ground cumin , 1 tbsp ground oregano
- 1/2 tsp ground cloves , 1 cup water
- 3 lbs beef eye of round or bottom round roast, all fat trimmed
- 2 1/2 teaspoons kosher salt , black pepper
- 1 tsp oil , 3 bay leaves

Instructions:

- o Place garlic, onion, lime juice, cumin, oregano, chipotles, cloves and water in a blender and puree until smooth.
- o Trim all the fat off meat, cut into 3-inch pieces. Season with 2 teaspoons salt and black pepper. Heat the pressure cooker on high (use saute button for Instant Pot), when hot add the oil and brown the meat, in batches on all side, about 5 minutes. Add the sauce from the blender and bay leaves, cover and cook on high pressure until the meat is tender and easily shreds with 2 forks, about 1 hour. (in my Instant Pot I cooked it 65

minutes). (If you're making this on the stove, simmer it on low at least 4 hours, adding more water as needed to make sure it doesn't dry out.)

o Once cooked and the meat is tender, remove the meat and place in a dish. Shred with two forks, and reserve the liquid for later (discard the bay leaf). Return the shredded meat to the pot, add 1/2 teaspoon salt or to taste, 1/2 tsp cumin and 1 1/2 cups of the reserved liquid.

Nutrition info per serving : Calories: 153 calories, Total Fat: 4.5g , Saturated Fat: g , Cholesterol: 44mg , Sodium: 334.5mg , Carbohydrates: 2g , Fiber: 0g , Sugar: 0g , Protein: 24g

Dinner
Instant Pot Cheesy Turkey Burger Macaroni

Prep+Cook time: 30 minutes, Servings: 8 , Smart points : 8

Ingredients

- 1 Tablespoon olive oil , 1 pound lean ground turkey
- 1 medium onion chopped , 1/2 teaspoon salt
- 1/4 teaspoon black pepper , 1/2 teaspoon dried thyme
- 1/4 cup ketchup , 2 cups elbow macaroni
- 3 cups beef stock , 8 oz Fontina cheese grated

Instructions

o Heat the olive oil on SAUTE mode with the pressure cooker's lid off. Place the turkey into the cooker and cook until it's browned, about 5 minutes.

- o Add the remaining ingredients, except for the cheese, to the cooker. Securely lock the lid and set on MANUAL for 6 minutes at HIGH pressure.
- o Perform a quick release to release the pressure. Add the shredded Fontina cheese and stir until it's melted and creamy. Serve immediately.

Nutrition info per serving : Calories: 332kcal, Carbohydrates: 24.6g, Protein: 23.3g, Fat: 15.8g

DAY 11
Break Fast
Double Chocolate Banana Bread
Prep+Cook time: 1 hr 10 mins, SmartPoints: 4, Servings: 8

Ingredients
- 1/2 cup butter softened & 1/2 cup brown sugar
- 1/4 cup white sugar & 1 large egg
- 2 teaspoons vanilla extract
- 3 medium bananas mashed - about 1 cup
- 1/4 cup sour cream & 1 cup all-purpose flour
- 1/2 cup cocoa powder & 1 teaspoon baking soda
- 1/2 teaspoon salt & 1 cup milk chocolate chips

Instructions
- Preheat oven to 350 degrees. Spray a 9x5x3 loaf pan with non-stick spray.
- Add the butter and sugars to a mixing bowl and mix until well combined.
- Beat in the egg, vanilla, banana, and sour cream.
- Stir in the flour, cocoa powder, baking soda, and salt.
- Pour mixture into prepared loaf pan.
- Sprinkle the top with chocolate chips and gently press them into the batter.
- Bake for 70 minutes or until a tester comes out clean. If you under bake this, the center will sink upon cooling.
- Let bread cool completely before cutting and serving.
- PLEASE NOTE: I baked this bread in a ceramic loaf pan. If you're using a glass or metal pan, your baking times may vary. Keep an eye on the bread and check with a tester before removing from the oven.

Nutrition info per serving : Calories 425 Calories from Fat 171, Total Fat 19g 29% , Saturated Fat 12g 60% , Cholesterol 60mg 20% , Sugars 39g , Protein 5g

Lunch
Macaroni and Cheese Recipe

Prep Time 5 mins //Cook Time 5 mins
Servings 8, **Points Values : 8**

Ingredients

- o 12 ounces whole wheat shell pasta
- o 4 cups low-fat and low-sodium chicken stock
- o 1 cup fat-free half and half
- o 6 slices Velveeta Original cheese slices
- o 1/4 cup Parmesan grated
- o 1/4 cup Fat-Free Cheddar shredded
- o 1 tablespoon margarine, 1 teaspoon garlic powder
- o 1 teaspoon black pepper , 1 1/2 teaspoon salt

Instructions

- Pour pasta, half and half, and chicken stock into Instant Pot liner and stir.
- Place lid on Instant Pot and set to seal. Choose manual and set to 5 minutes.
- Allow to come to pressure, cook, and when complete NPR (natural pressure release) for 2 minutes. Release remaining pressure, and set to saute.
- Add in cheese slices, margarine, garlic powder, salt, and pepper and mix well. Stir consistently until completely melted.
- Turn off saute feature and taste. May add salt and pepper to taste.

Nutrition Facts Per Serving Amount Per Serving (8 g) / Calories 243 Calories from Fat 45 / Total Fat 5g / Saturated Fat 1g / Cholesterol 8mg

Dinner
Instant Pot Chicken Cacciatore

Prep+Cook time:35 minutes, 4 servings, 3 Freestyle Points
Ingredients:
- 4 chicken thighs, with the bone, skin removed
- kosher salt and fresh pepper to taste
- olive oil spray
- 1/2 can (14 oz) crushed tomatoes (Tuttorosso my favorite!)
- 1/2 cup diced onion , 1/4 cup diced red bell pepper
- 1/2 cup diced green bell pepper
- 1/2 teaspoon dried oregano , 1 bay leaf
- 2 tablespoons chopped basil or parsley for topping

Instructions:

o Season chicken with salt and pepper on both side.
o Press saute on the Instant Pot, lightly spray with oil and brown chicken on both sides a few minutes. Set aside.
o Spray with a little more oil and add onions and peppers. Sauté until soften and golden, 5 minutes.
o Pour tomatoes over the chicken and vegetables, add oregano, bay leaf, salt and pepper, give it a quick stir and cover.
o Cook high pressure 25 minutes; natural release.
o Remove bay leaf, garnish with parsley and serve over pasta, squasta or whatever you wish!

Nutrition info per serving : 133 caloriesTotal Fat: 3g, Saturated Fat: 0.5g, Cholesterol: 57mg, Sodium: 273mg, Protein: 14g

DAY 12

Break Fast
Italian Pulled Pork Ragu

Total Time: varies / Servings : 10, Serving Size: 1/2 cup sauce
Points Values: 1
Ingredients:
- o 18 oz pork tenderloin , 1 teaspoon kosher salt
- o black pepper to taste & 1 tsp olive oil
- o 5 cloves garlic, smashed with the side of a knife
- o 1 (28 oz can) crushed tomatoes (I love Tuttorosso)
- o 1 small jar roasted red peppers, drained (7 oz jar)
- o 2 sprigs fresh thyme , 2 bay leaves
- o 1 tbsp chopped fresh parsley, divided

Instructions:

- Season pork with salt and pepper. Press saute button to warm, add oil and garlic and saute until golden brown, 1 to 1 1/2 minutes; remove with a slotted spoon.
- Add pork and brown about 2 minutes on each side.
- Add the remaining ingredients and garlic, reserving half of the parsley.
- Cook high pressure 45 minutes. Natural release, remove bay leaves, shred the pork with 2 forks and top with remaining parsley.
- Serve over your favorite pasta.

Nutrition Facts Per Serving Calories: 93 calories / Total Fat: 1.5g /Saturated Fat: g /Cholesterol: 33mg

Lunch
Instant Pot Sunday Pot Roast

Prep+Cook time: 1 hr 45 mins, Servings: 4, SmartPoints : 7

Ingredients

- 3 lbs beef chuck roast (fat trimmed) & 1 tbp olive oil
- 2 packets onion soup mix
- 1 large onion (roughly chopped)
- 3 tbsp Worcestershire sauce
- 1 1/2 cups fat free beef broth
- 3 large carrots (cut into large chunks)
- 1 lb Yukon gold potatoes (cut into large chunks)
- Salt and pepper to taste

Instructions

o Season both sides of roast with salt and pepper. In a small bowl, whisk together the broth, onion soup mix, and Worcestershire sauce.

o Set instant pot to saute. When hot, add in oil. Add in meat and saute on all sides,about 1-2 minutes per side.

o Top meat with potatoes, onions and carrots, and prepared sauce.

o Turn off saute. Cover Instant Pot with lid, and switch to manual setting. Set for 70 minutes on high pressure. Allow to naturally release for 10 minutes, then quick release whatever pressure is left.

o Remove from instant pot, shred and serve with vegetables.

Nutrition info per serving : Calories 389 Calories from Fat 117 , Total Fat 13g 20% , Saturated Fat 4.1g 21% , Cholesterol 150mg 50%, Sodium 865mg 36% , Potassium 806mg 23% , Total Carbohydrates 20g 7% , Dietary Fiber 3.2g 13% , Sugars 4.5g , Protein 48g

Dinner
Barbacoa Beef (Pressure Cooker or Instant Pot)

Prep+Cook time:1 hour 20 minutes, 9 Servings,
3 Freestyle Points

Ingredients:

- 5 cloves garlic , 1/2 medium onion
- 1 lime juice
- 2-4 tbsp chiptoles in adobo sauce (to taste)
- 1 tbsp ground cumin , 1 tbsp ground oregano
- 1/2 tsp ground cloves , 1 cup water
- 3 lbs beef eye of round or bottom round roast, all fat trimmed
- 2 1/2 teaspoons kosher salt , black pepper
- 1 tsp oil , 3 bay leaves

Instructions:

o Place garlic, onion, lime juice, cumin, oregano, chipotles, cloves and water in a blender and puree until smooth.

o Trim all the fat off meat, cut into 3-inch pieces. Season with 2 teaspoons salt and black pepper. Heat the pressure cooker on high (use saute button for Instant Pot), when hot add the oil and brown the meat, in batches on all side, about 5 minutes. Add the sauce from the blender and bay leaves, cover and cook on high pressure until the meat is tender and easily shreds with 2 forks, about 1 hour. (in my Instant Pot I cooked it 65 minutes). (If you're making this on the stove, simmer it on low at least 4 hours, adding more water as needed to make sure it doesn't dry out.)

- o Once cooked and the meat is tender, remove the meat and place in a dish. Shred with two forks, and reserve the liquid for later (discard the bay leaf). Return the shredded meat to the pot, add 1/2 teaspoon salt or to taste, 1/2 tsp cumin and 1 1/2 cups of the reserved liquid.

Nutrition info per serving : Calories: 153 caloriesTotal Fat: 4.5g, Saturated Fat: g, Cholesterol: 44mg, Sodium: 334.5mg, Carbohydrates: 2g, Protein: 24g

DAY 13

Break Fast
Whole Wheat Pancakes

Prep+Cook time:15 minutes, 7 Servings, Smart Points : 5

Ingredients:

- 2 cups white whole wheat flour
- 4 1/2 tsp baking powder , 1/2 tsp kosher salt
- 2 tsp ground cinnamon , 2 tsp sugar
- 2 large eggs , 2 cups + 2 tbsp fat free milk
- 2 tsp vanilla extract , cooking spray

Instructions:

o Mix all dry ingredients in a bowl. Add wet ingredients to the mixing bowl and mix well with a spoon until there are no more dry spots; don't over-mix.

o Heat a large skillet on medium heat. Lightly spray oil to coat and pour 1/4 cup of pancake batter. When the pancake starts to bubble, you may add your fruit if you wish. When the bubbles settle and the edges begin to set, flip the pancakes. Repeat with the remainder of the batter. Makes 14 pancakes.

Nutrition info per serving : Calories: 172 calories , Total Fat: 2g , Saturated Fat: g ,Cholesterol: 5mg ,Sodium: 561mg, Carbohydrates: 31.5g , Fiber: 5g , Sugar: 2.5g, Protein: 9g

DAY 14

Break Fast
Pumpkin Pie Oatmeal

Prep+Cook Time 10 minute, Servings 2, Smart Points : 5

Ingredients

- 1 cup Old fashioned Rolled Oats
- 1 1/2 cups Unsweetened almond milk , vanilla or plain
- 1/4 cup Pumpkin puree , 1/2 tsp Cinnamon
- 1/2 tsp Pumpkin Pie Spice , 1/2 tsp Vanilla
- Toppings of choice (optional): walnuts, pecans, maple syrup, sugar free maple syrup, brown sugar, stevia

Instructions

- o In a small pan, add oats and unsweetened almond milk. Cook over medium heat, bring to a boil, and then reduce to simmer and stir occasionally for about 4-5 minutes, or until desired consistency is reached. Add pumpkin puree, vanilla, cinnamon, and pumpkin pie spice. Cook for another 1-2 minutes. Serve and top with desired toppings to add a bit of sweetness, or nuts for a bit of crunch.

Nutrition info per serving : 115 Calories, 3g of fat, 0g saturated fat, 17g carbohydrates, 4g fiber, 2g sugar, 4g protein.

Lunch
Instant Pot Chicken Tikka Masala with Cauliflower and Peas

Total Time:25 minutes, Servings : 6, Serving Size: 3/4 cup
Points Values: 5

Ingredients:

o 1 1/2 pounds skinless, boneless chicken thighs, cubed
o 1 1/2 teaspoon kosher salt
o 1/2 tablespoon ghee, butter or coconut oil for df
o 1/2 chopped onion
o 3 cloves garlic, minced
o 1 teaspoon grated ginger root
o 1 teaspoon ground coriander
o 1 teaspoon cumin
o 1/2 teaspoon turmeric
o 1/2 teaspoon garam masala
o 1/4 teaspoon cayenne pepper
o 1/4 teaspoon ground cardamom
o 14 ounce can diced tomatoes, drained
o 2 cups cauliflower florets
o 1/2 cup frozen peas
o 1/2 cup full fat canned coconut milk
o 1/4 cup fresh cilantro leaves, for serving

Instructions:

- Season chicken with 1 teaspoon salt.
- Press saute button and melt the butter, add onion, garlic, ginger and 6 spices (from coriander to cardamom) and

saute until the vegetables are soft and the spices are fragrant, about 2 to 3 minutes.

- Add the tomatoes and use an immersion to blend until smooth (or blend in the blender), add the chicken, remaining 1/2 teaspoon salt and stir, cook high pressure 15 minutes.
- Quick release, add the cauliflower and peas and cook 2 minutes on high pressure.
- Quick release, stir in coconut milk and serve garnished with cilantro.

Nutrition Facts Per Serving Calories: 226 calories / Total Fat: 10g / Saturated Fat: g / Cholesterol: 3mg

Dinner
Lamb Curry Stew with Chickpeas and Artichoke Hearts

Prep+Cook time: 40 min, Servings: 4, 5 Freestyle Points

Ingredients

- 2 pounds uncooked lean and trimmed lamb leg, loin, or stew meat, cut into 1-inch chunks
- 1 teaspoon kosher salt
- 1/2 teaspoon black pepper
- 1/2 teaspoon of curry powder
- 1 tablespoon olive oil
- 1 large uncooked onion, chopped
- 1 clove garlic clove, minced
- 1 cup canned beef broth
- 14 1/2 ounces fire roasted diced tomatoes (canned), undrained
- 15 ounces chickpeas (canned), drained

- 14 ounces quarted artichoke hearts (canned), drained
- 1/3 cup small green manzanilla olives
- 2 tsp ginger root, freshly grated
- 1 tablespoon curry powder
- 1 teaspoon garam masala
- 1/2 tsp ground cinnamon
- 1 Tbsp fresh lemon juice

Instructions

- Toss lamb pieces with salt, pepper, and 1/2 tablespoon of curry. Heat tablespoon of olive oil in pressure cooker pot. Brown lamb on high saute, working in two batches. Remove lamb from the pot and place in a bowl.
- Saute onion and garlic until the onion starts to carmelize.
- After the onions are brown around the edges, pour in the cup of broth and scrape off any stuck on seasonings from the lamb and incorporate in with the onions. Your pressure cooker may not work properly if you have browned/burned on food on the bottom of the pot
- Add the lamb + any juices back to pot. Add the rest of the ingredients, except for the lemon juice, and stir to mix.
- Cook on high pressure for 12 minutes. Use quick pressure release.
- Stir in lemon juice and let stand for 5 minutes for flavors to blend.

Notes : If you like your curry spicy, feel free to increase the amount of curry you use, and/or add 1/4 teaspoon of cayenne pepper. Serve over Jasmine or Basmati Rice - 3 SP for 1/2 cup of cooked rice.

DAY 15
Break Fast
Apple Pie Bubble Up

Prep+Cook Time 32 minutes, Servings 8, Smart Points : 5

Ingredients
- 2 large tart apples *granny smith or honey crisp- cored , peeled, and roughly chopped into small pieces
- 1 1/2 tsp cinnamon + a little extra for topping
- 2 tsp pure vanilla or vanilla extract
- 1/4 cup brown sugar + 2 tbs for the topping
- 1/4 cup nonfat sour cream , 1/2 cup water
- 1 tbs butter , melted, for topping
- pinch of salt , for topping
- 1/2 cup old fashioned oats , for topping
- 1 7.5 oz can refrigerated buttermilk biscuits , each biscuit cut into eighths (Pillsbury makes these in four packs, but recently I have seen store brands carry these in a single can- If you cannot find these smaller cans. You can get a regular pack of buttermilk biscuits and weigh 7.5 oz out)
- Cooking Spray

Instructions
- o Preheat the oven to 350 degrees. In a large mixing bowl add chopped apples, 1/4 cup brown sugar, water, vanilla, cinnamon, and sour cream. Mix until combined. In a medium saucepan add the apple mixture and cook over medium-high heat until the apples are softened. While apples are cooking grab a small bowl add oats, 2 tablespoons brown sugar,

melted butter, a few more shakes of cinnamon, and a pinch of salt. Mix well. Spray a 3 quart casserole dish with cooking spray, add the cut up biscuit pieces and the top with the warmed apple pie filling. Lightly stir into the biscuits. Sprinkle the oat topping mix on top. Place into the oven for about 22 minutes or until the top is lightly browned and biscuits are bubbled up.

Nutrition info per serving : 152 calories 2.5g fat. 29g carbs. fiber 1g. sugars 13g. protein 3g

Lunch
Instant Pot Sausage Cabbage Bowl with Quinoa

Prep+Cook time: 52 mins, Smart Points: 5, Serves 6

Ingredients

- 2 tsp olive oil
- 1 lb. hot or sweet Italian chicken sausage (raw)
- 1 yellow onion chopped & 3 garlic cloves
- 1 tsp paprika & 1 tsp dried oregano
- 3/4 tsp salt & 1/2 tsp ground pepper
- 1 1/4 cup low sodium chicken broth
- 1 cup canned petite diced tomatoes
- 1/2 cup dry quinoa
- 1 3/4 lb. cabbage, thinly sliced (about 12 cups)
- 1/4 cup minced Italian parsley
- Salt and pepper, to taste

Instructions

- o Set Instant Pot to Saute setting. Add the olive oil and allow to heat for 30 seconds. Add the chicken sausage (squeezed out of casings) and onion, and cook, breaking up the sausage with a wooden spoon, until the sausage is browned, about 5 minutes. Stir in the garlic, paprika, oregano, salt and pepper.
- o Add the chicken broth and diced tomatoes, and stir to combine.
- o Put the lid on the Instant Pot, close the steam vent and set to HIGH pressure using the manual setting. Decrease the time to 12 minutes. (It will take about 15 minutes for the Instant Pot to reach pressure.)
- o Once the time is expired, carefully use the quick release valve (it may sputter a bit) to release the steam.
- o Stir in the quinoa and pile the cabbage on top (don't stir it in). Put the lid on the Instant Pot again, close the steam vent and set to HIGH pressure. Decrease the time to 3 minutes. Release the steam using the quick release valve.
- o Stir in the parsley and season to taste. Serve.

Nutrition info per serving : Calories 233.5 cal Calories from fat 72, Total Fat 8.9g 14% , Saturated Fat 2.3g 12% , Cholesterol 55.0mg 18% , Sodium 874.9mg 36% , Carbohydrate 26.0g 9% , Dietary Fiber 6.4g 26% , Sugars 8.9g , Protein 16.7g

Dinner
Instant Pot Skinny Steak Soup
Prep/Cook time: 25 minutes, 3 Freestyle Points

Ingredients

- 1 lb Steak, or stew meat , fat trimmed
- 1 Onion diced & 2 Carrots diced
- 2 Celery Stalk diced
- 4 sweet peppers, diced (or 1 large bell pepper)
- 8 oz mushrooms, cremini, button sliced thin
- 2 tbsp garlic powder & 2 tsp celtic sea salt
- 2 tsp oregano & 1 tsp thyme
- 1 bay leaf & 1 cup crushed tomatoes
- 2 cups beef stock & 2 cups water

Instructions

o Set Instant pot to saute (or heat a large stock pot to medium).
o Add stew meat and brown.
o Add onion, celery, pepper, carrots, and cook until softened. Add mushrooms, cook until soft.
o Add spices, salt, water, and stock and cover instant pot, setting to seal. (or cover with lid and set to low if cooking on stove.)
o Cook on soup setting for 15 minutes (if cooking on stovetop, cook on low for 1 hour).
o Release steam and serve hot.

Nutrition info per serving : Calories: 364 Saturated Fat: 7g Cholesterol: 69mg Sodium: 431mg Carbohydrates: 24g Fiber: 6g Sugar: 12g Protein: 30g

DAY 16

Break Fast

One Point Weight Watcher Pancakes

Prep Time 10 mins // Cook Time 10 mins

Servings: 14 pancakes, **Points Values:1**

Ingredients

- o 2 over-ripe bananas mashed , 2 egg whites
- o 1 cup of fat-free plain greek yogurt
- o 1/2 cup of fat-free milk
- o 1 teaspoon of pure vanilla extract
- o 1 cup of all-purpose flour
- o 2 teaspoons of baking powder
- o 1/2 teaspoon of cinnamon

Instructions

- Preheat a nonstick electric skillet to 325 degrees.
- In a medium sized bowl, combine mashed bananas, egg whites, greek yogurt, milk and vanilla extract. Whisk until well combines.
- In a larger bowl, combine flour, baking powder and cinnamon and whisk.
- Stir wet ingredient into dry ingredients.
- Pour 1/4 cup of batter onto hot skillet and cook until golden brown.

Nutrition Facts Per Serving Calories 40, Sodium 58mg, Total Carbohydrates 10g

Lunch
Weight Watchers Buffalo Chicken Wings

Prep Time 5 mins// Cook Time11 mins
Servings: 4, **Points Values: 3**

Ingredients

- o 2 lbs . 2 large breasts partially defrosted chicken breast cut into strips (I've also used frozen chicken breasts, please see below)
- o 1/2 cup Franks Red Hot Sauce & 1 tsp . cayenne pepper
- o 1 tsp . salt & 2 tbsp . butter & 1 tsp . pepper
- o 1/4 cup Franks Red Hot Sauce for coating

Instructions

- Turn the Instant Pot to saute to melt the butter. When it is melted add in the chicken, salt, pepper, and cayenne pepper. Mix the chicken so that each piece is seasoned.
- I've also placed frozen chicken breasts in the Instant Pot, along with the other ingredients (minus butter), and cooked for 16 minutes. I cube the chicken after it's cooked and continue with the recipe.
- Add 1/2 cup hot sauce then stir the chicken so that it is coated.
- Lock the lid into place and turn the steam valve to sealing. Using the manual setting cook on high pressure for 8 minutes. If your chicken is fully defrosted cook for 7 minutes. I used partially defrosted chicken because it is easier to cut. Release the pressure using the quick release method.

- In a hurry? Drizzle warm sauce before serving and skip the last step!
- Using tongs, remove the chicken from the Instant Pot and place on a baking sheet lined with aluminum foil. Brush the chicken with the additional 1/4 cup hot sauce. Thicken the sauce by placing under the broiler for 3 minutes. Turn the chicken over and repeat on the other side. Let the chicken cool 5 minutes before serving. Goat cheese is tastes amazing spread on top.

Nutrition Facts Per Serving   Weight Watchers, 1 Serving (Recipe Serves 4), 3 Freestyle Smart Points

Dinner
Mexican Pot Pork Carnitas
Prep/Cook: 1 hour 10 min, Servings: 11, 3 SmartPoints

Ingredients

- 2 1/2 lbs boneless pork shoulder blade roast, trimmed
- 3/4 cup low sodium chicken broth
- 1/2 tsp sazon, homemade works too
- 2-3 chipotle peppers in adobo sauce, to taste
- 6 garlic cloves cut into sliver
- 1/4 tsp dry adobo seasoning, Goya can be used
- 1 1/2 tsp cumin , black pepper to taste
- 1/4 tsp dry oregano , 2 bay leaves , 2 tsp kosher salt

Instructions

- o Use salt and pepper to season pork. Add port in a large skillet and brown all sides on high heat for about 5 minutes. Then, remove from heat and let cool.
- o Make a cut about 1-inch deep in the meat with a sharp knife, and insert the garlic slivers. You can do this all

over. Once again, season the entire pork with sazon, cumin, oregano, adobo and garlic powder.

o In the crockpot, add chipotle, pour chicken broth, peppers, and mix. Add bay leaves before placing pork in the Instant Pot. Cook covered in a the pressure cooker by setting on high pressure with the meat button for 50 minutes. When the pressure is released, shred pork with two forks and combine well with the remaining juices at the bottom. Adjust cumin, after removing bay leaves. Add adobo and mix well.

Nutrition info per serving : Calories: 160 , Fat: 7 g , Sat Fat: 3 g , Carb: 1 g , Fiber: 0 g , Protein: 20 g , Sugar: 0 g

DAY 17

Break Fast
Bacon Bell Pepper Frittata

Prep+Cook Time 30 minutes, Servings 4, SmartPoints : 4

Ingredients

- 1/2 cup 1% milk (or skim milk) & 8 eggs
- 3/4 cup shredded Colby Jack Cheese made with 2% milk
- 7 slices center cut bacon chopped
- 1 medium red bell pepper chopped
- 1/2 onion chopped & 2 cloves garlic minced
- pinch of salt & cooking spray
- green onions chopped (for garnish, optional)

Instructions

o Preheat oven to 350 degrees. In a large skillet over medium-high heat add bacon and cook for a few minutes before adding the pepper, onion, and garlic.

o Cook all together until bacon is crisp and onions and pepper are caramelized, about 6-8 minutes.

o While the bacon mixture is cooking, add eggs, milk, and pinch of salt into a medium bowl and whisk together. When the bacon mixture is done cooking add the shredded cheese and the bacon mixture to the eggs and stir until combined.

o Pour into a 9 inch pie plate sprayed with cooking spray. Bake for 30 minutes.

o Remove from oven, slice into 4 servings, and enjoy!

Nutrition info per serving : 235 Calories 11g fat, 5g saturated fat, 6g carbohydrates, 1g fiber, 3g sugar, 20g protein

Lunch
Chickpea Sweet Potato Stew

Prep+Cook time:4 hours 15 mins, 6 servings, Smart Points : 3

Ingredients

- 1 medium yellow onion, chopped
- 2 15 oz cans garbanzo beans, drained
- 1 pound sweet potatoes, peeled and chopped
- 1 tablespoon garlic, minced
- 1/2 teaspoon Kosher salt
- 1/4 teaspoon coarse ground black pepper
- 1 teaspoon ground ginger
- 1 1/2 teaspoons ground cumin
- 1 teaspoon ground coriander
- 1/4 teaspoon ground cinnamon
- 4 cups vegetable broth, fat free
- 4 cups fresh baby spinach

Instructions:

- Place the onions in a microwave safe dish and microwave 2 to 3 minutes.
- Add all the ingredients to your slow cooker except the spinach.
- Cook on low for 6-7 hours or on high for 3-4 hours.
- Add in the spinach leaves and stir.
- Cook an additional 15 minutes on high.

Instant Pot:

- Add the ingredients together except for the spinach and cook on high pressure for 8 minutes.
- Quick release, stir in the spinach and let it sit 2 minutes covered, until wilted.

o (You can also sweat the garlic and onions first, but if doing so add a teaspoon of olive oil. This will give you the best results)

Nutrition info per serving : Calories: 165 calories, Total Fat: 2.2g, Saturated Fat: 1.4g, Cholesterol: 0mg, Sodium: 751mg, Carbohydrates: 32.3g , Fiber: 6.2g , Sugar: 5.4g , Protein: 6.3g

Dinner
Instant Pot Asian Chicken

Prep+Cook time: 32 minutes, Serving 4, FreeStyle Points: 2

Ingredients

- 1 pound chicken breast meat (she used tenderloins)
- 2 tablepoons low sodium soy sauce
- 2 tablespoons low sodium chicken broth
- 2 tablepoons Hoisin sauce , 1 tablespoon honey
- 1 teaspoon minced garlic , 1/4 teaspoon chili-garlic sauce
- 1 teaspoon cornstarch , 2 teaspoon water
- green onions (sliced - optional) , shredded carrots (optional)
- 1 teaspoon minced or grated ginger root

Instructions

o Put chicken in bottom on instant pot liner. Mix soy sauce, chicken broth, hoisin sauce, honey, garlic, ginger,chili-garlic sauce together and pour over chicken.

- Cook on slow cooker setting (venting left open) on high for 2 hours or low for 4 hours. (she did hers on high for 2 hours).
- Remove chicken, place on board and shred with forks. Mix the cornstarch with 2T water. Pour remaining pot juices into a small saucepan, add in the cornstarch mixture and bring to a gentle boil for a few minutes until it thickens. Put shredded chicken in a mixing bowl and add warm sauce, stir.
- Makes four 4-ounce servings. I put 2 oz. of chicken into each half of a pita pocket, added some chopped lettuce, shredded carrot and the green onion.

Nutrition info per serving : Calories 0 Total Fat 0g Saturated Fat 0g Cholesterol 0mg Sodium 0mg Fiber 0g Sugar 0g Protein 0g

DAY 18
Easy Braised Chicken Drumsticks in Tomatillo Sauce

Prep+Cook time:30 minutes/pressure cooker,
Smart Points: 3, Servings: 6

Ingredients:

- 6 chicken drumsticks, on the bone, skin removed (24 oz)
- 1 tbsp cider vinegar & 1 tsp kosher salt
- 1/8 tsp black pepper & 1 teaspoon dried oregano
- 1 teaspoon olive oil
- 1 1/2 cups jarred tomatillo sauce (I used Frontera)
- 1/4 cup chopped cilantro, divided
- 1 jalapeno, halved and seeded

Instructions:

- o Season chicken with vinegar, salt, pepper and oregano. Marinate a few hours if time permits.
- o Set the Instant Pot to saute, when hot add the oil and the chicken to brown on both sides, about 4 minutes on each side.
- o Add the tomatillo salsa, 2 tablespoons of the cilantro and jalapeno, cover and cook on high pressure 20 minutes, until the chicken is tender. When the pressure releases, garnish with cilantro and serve over rice if desired.

Nutrition info per serving : Calories: 161 calories , Total Fat: 5g, Saturated Fat: 1g , Cholesterol: 101mg , Sodium: 736mg , Carbohydrates: 5g , Fiber: 0g , Sugar: 2g , Protein: 22g

Lunch
Instant Pot Jalapeno Dip

Prep Time 5 mins //Cook Time 15 mins Servings : 24
Points Values: 1

Ingredients

- o 1 Package fat free cream cheese
- o 1 cup fat free shredded cheddar cheese
- o 1/2 cup fat free sour cream
- o ½ cup shredded/diced chicken & ¼ cup diced jalapenos
- o ¼ cup diced green onions & ½ tsp cumin

For garnish:
- o A few sliced jalapenos
- o Sprinkle of pepper & Sprinkle of bread crumbs

Instructions

- Combine cream cheese, cheddar cheese, chicken, diced jalapenos, green onions, cumin, and pepper in the basin of your Instant Pot.
- Seal, set time to 5 minutes, and cook on "manual".
- Vent your cooker, open the lid, and stir in your sour cream until evenly blended.
- Pour into a serving dish and top with extra cheese, jalapenos, and bread crumbs.

Nutrition Facts Per Serving Per Serving: 80 calories; 6.6 g fat; 0.7 g carbohydrates; 4.7 g protein; 24 mg cholesterol; 137 mg sodium

Dinner
Weight Watchers Beef Gyros In The Instant Pot

Prep+Cook time: 25 mins, Servings: 6 , 8 Smart Points

Ingredients

- 2 lbs beef roast thinly sliced I've also used loin flap meat and it's so easy to slice and cook!
- 3 cloves minced garlic & 1 tbsp dried parsley
- 1 tsp black pepper , 1 tsp salt
- 1/2 cup vegetable broth , 1 red onion thinly sliced
- 1 tbsp lemon juice & 4 tbsp oil olive, coconut, avocado, etc
- 1 tsp apple cider vinegar optional , 1 tsp olive oil optional

Toppings

- Pitas or Naan bread or Flat Out pitas I love the Flat Out pitas the best!
- Sliced carrots , Sliced onions , Sliced cucumbers , Lettuce
- Feta or goat cheese optional, use container to measure

Tzatziki Sauce:
- 2 tbsp fresh dill & 1 cup plain Greek yogurt
- 1/2 cup cucumber peeled seeded and chopped
- 1 clove minced garlic , 1 tsp salt and pepper

Instructions

- o Turn Instant Pot on saute and let the pan warn up. When it's warm, add oil to the bottom of the pan and let it get hot.
- o Add meat, seasoning, garlic, and onion to Instant Pot. Sear and let onions soften for 3-5 minutes
- o Pour lemon juice and broth over the meat. Give the meat a quick stir, then lock lid into place. Turn the steam valve to sealing. Using the Meat/Stew preset cook the gyro meat for 9 minutes. Let the pressure naturally release for 3 minutes before releasing the remaining pressure using the quick release method.
- o While the gyro meat is cooking mix together the Tzatziki sauce and slice your vegetable toppings. For added flavor drizzle apple cider vinegar and olive oil over vegetables.
- o To make your gyro layer the lettuce at the bottom of the pita or naan bread. Then add your meat, toppings, and sauce. This will keep the pita or naan from getting soggy.

Nutrition info per serving : Calories: 535kcal, Carbohydrates: 27.1g, Protein: 54.5g, Fat: 22.7g, Saturated Fat: 6.1g

DAY 19
Break Fast
Instant Pot Egg Salad

Prep+Cook time: 35 minutes, Servings: 6, SmartPoints : 3

Ingredients
- 12 large eggs , finely chopped
- ½ cup (125g) full fat mayonnaise
- ½ tablespoon (7.5ml) unseasoned rice vinegar
- ½ tablespoon (7.5g) dijon mustard
- ½ teaspoon cumin , ground
- 1 (66g) dill pickle or cornichon , finely diced
- 3 stalks (32g) green onions , finely sliced
- 2 ribs (146g) celery (optional) , finely diced (omit if you prefer non-crunchy egg salad)
- 6 stems (10g) fresh dill , finely chopped
- Kosher salt and ground black pepper to taste
- No-stick cooking spray

Instructions
- o Important Step - Spray Pan: Apply cooking spray all over the pan. For easier removal, line the bottom of the pan with parchment paper.
- o Crack Eggs: Crack 12 large raw eggs into the pre-sprayed pan.
- o Pressure Cook Egg Loaf: Pour 1 cup (250ml) cold water and place a steamer rack in Instant Pot Pressure Cooker. Carefully layer the pan of cracked raw eggs on top.Close lid and pressure cook at High Pressure for 5 minutes + 9 minutes Natural Release. Open the lid carefully.

- Prepare Remaining Ingredients: While the egg loaf is pressure cooking, prepare remaining ingredients.
- Chop Egg Loaf: Remove egg loaf from Instant Pot & set aside on a chopping board to cool. Once cool to touch, finely chop the egg loaf. Allow the chopped eggs to cool to room temperature.
- Make Salad Dressing: In a large mixing bowl, add ½ cup (125g) mayonnaise, finely diced ingredients (pickle, green onions, and celery), ½ tsp ground cumin, ½ tbsp (7.5g) dijon mustard, ½ tbsp (7.5ml) unseasoned rice vinegar, and finely chopped hard-boiled eggs. Mix well with a silicone spatula. Drizzle in the finely chopped fresh dill and mix one more time with a silicone spatula.
- Adjust Seasoning & Chill in Fridge: Taste the salad and season with more kosher salt & fresh ground black pepper to taste. You will want the egg salad to be a little on the salty side because chilling it in the refrigerator will decrease the perception of seasoning. Cover & place egg salad in the refrigerator for at least 3 hours.

Lunch
Instant Pot Salsa Chicken

Prep+Cook time: 30 minutes, Servings: 6 , Smart points : 3

Ingredients

- 1 Tablespoon olive oil
- 1 Tablespoon garlic minced
- 1 medium onion chopped
- 1 pound boneless chicken breast
- 1/2 cup low-sodium chicken broth
- 15oz can sweet corn drained and rinsed
- 15oz can black beans drained and rinsed
- 1 jar salsa of your choice
- 1 packet taco seasoning
- 1 pouch Uncle Ben's brown rice

Instructions

- Heat the Instant Pot using the SAUTE mode. Once it's hot, add the olive oil, garlic and onion. Cook until the onion is translucent and the garlic is fragrant.
- Add the chicken breasts over the onion mixture. Sprinkle the package of taco seasoning over the chicken breasts. Add the salsa, corn and black beans to the Instant Pot.
- Using MANUAL mode, cook the salsa chicken on HIGH pressure for 10 minutes. You can do a quick release of the pressure, or wait and use a natural release. Once the Instant Pot is finished cooking, take the chicken out and

shred the chicken. Add the chicken back to the Instant Pot and stir to combine.

o   Serve immediately. You can serve this over rice or in taco shells - it's totally up to you. We ate it over rice and it was wonderful!

Nutrition info per serving : Calories: 332kcal, Carbohydrates: 37.7g, Protein: 23.8g, Fat: 10.7g, Saturated Fat: 2.6g, Cholesterol: 48.4mg, Fiber: 8.3g, Sugar: 5.7g

Dinner
Instant Pot Honey Garlic Chicken

Prep+Cook Time: 30 Min, Servings: 6, Freestyle Points: 3

Ingredients

- 2 lbs. boneless skinless chicken thighs
- 1/3 cup low sodium soy sauce
- 1/4 cup ketchup (no sugar added)
- 3 tbsp. honey & 4 garlic cloves minced

Instructions

o   Add the chicken thighs to the bottom of the slow cooker. Mix together the remaining ingredients to create the sauce.

o   Pour over the chicken and stir. Cook on manual mode for 20 minutes. Once it is finished cooking, use the quick release.

o   Shred the chicken using two forks. If needed, you can thicken up the sauce using a touch of cornstarch,

although normally I don't need it. It will depend on the
liquid content of your chicken thighs,

Nutrition info per serving : Calories 234 , Calories from Fat 1 ,
Total Fat 6g , Sugars 11g , Protein 30g

DAY 20
Break Fast
Pressure Cooker Pumpkin Puree Recipe

Prep Time 5 mins, Cook Time 18 mins, **Points Values:0**

Ingredients
- 1 small sugar (pie) pumpkin (about 2 - 3 pounds)

Instructions

- Add steamer rack to InstantPot Pressure cooker.
- Add 1 cup water to pressure cooker.
- Place pumpkin on rack inside pressure cooker and make sure the lid seals. If the stem is too tall, trim stem until lid seals properly.
- Seal pressure cooker cover and cook on HIGH pressure for 13 minutes.
- Your InstantPot pressure cooker will take some time to build up the pressure and temperature inside.
- After the 13 minute cooking time finishes, allow your InstantPot to release the pressure naturally for at least 10 minutes. Then if you want to release it manually, go ahead. Or, just let it completely release on its own.
- Once the pressure is released, remove the cover and carefully lift out the rack, being careful not to drop the pumpkin which will be very hot.
- Place pumpkin on a cutting board and cut in half.
- Scoop out seeds and pumpkin goop. Feel free to rinse and drain pumpkin seeds for later use.

- Peel cooked pumpkin from the skin and add to Vitamix or other high-powered blender or food processor. Process to desired consistency.
- Scoop out fresh pumpkin puree and store in airtight container in the refrigerator.

Nutrition Facts Per Serving Amount Per Serving (1 /2 cup), Calories 38 Calories from Fat 3 , Total Carbohydrates 9.1g 3% ,Dietary Fiber 3.3g 13% ,Protein 1.2g

Lunch
Instant Pot Shrimp Recipes
Points Values: 5
Ingredients

o ¼ cup butter , 1 cup rice
o 2Tbsp minced garlic , 1½ cups water or broth
o 1 can black beans, rinsed and drained
o 1lb Frozen Shrimp (raw or cooked, just make sure it's frozen)
o 15-20 drops Young Living Lime Vitality Essential Oil
o Fresh or freeze dried cilantro , salt and pepper to taste

Instructions

- Set Instant Pot to "saute" and melt butter
- Add rice and cook until brown. Add garlic, salt, and pepper and cook until fragrant
- Add water and lime oil, then beans and shrimp
- Set Instant Pot to manual and cook for 5 minutes
- Release the pressure manually and serve dish topped with cilantro

Dinner
Weight Watchers Crockpot Pork Carnitas

Prep+Cook time: 8 hrs 10 mins, Servings: 8 , Smart Points : 2

Ingredients

- 2 lbs pork tenderloin Smithfield, we purchased ours at Walmart, it was about 2 pounds
- 1 cup Green Chile Salsa , 1 can Rotel , 2 Onions
- 2 Bay Leaves , 2 t Cayenne Pepper
- 2 tbs. Chili Powder
- Optional for taste: Salt and Pepper and sour cream

Instructions

o Slice one onion into thick slices and line the bottom of your crock pot with them. Dice the other onion and set aside for a topping.

o Place pork tenderloin on top of the onions and sprinkle your spices (and place bay leaves) on the pork.

o Pour 1/2 bottle of salsa, entire can of Rotel, and diced onions on and around pork.

o Cook on low for 5-8 hours, depending on the size of your tenderloin.

o Pull pork out and shred it, then add it back into the crockpot.Serve with the rest of the bottle of green chile salsa, warm flour or corn tortillas, diced onions, and sour cream.

Instant Pot Pork Carnitas Instructions

- Add pork tenderloin and other ingredients into the Instant Pot. Pressure cook on high pressure for 8 minutes (I did this for a 2 pound tenderloin), then let pressure naturally release for 15 minutes.
- Pull out the pork and shred it, then place it back to the Instant Pot.

Nutrition info per serving : Serving: 1g, Calories: 172kcal, Carbohydrates: 6g, Protein: 24g, Fat: 4g

DAY 21

Break Fast

Chocolate Donuts – Weight Watchers Freestyle

Prep+Cook time: 52 mins, Serving: 12 Donuts
Smart points : 3

Ingredients
- 1 box Pillsbury sugar free brownie mix
- 8 oz. Coke Zero & 2 egg whites
- 2 tablespoons powdered sugar

Instructions
- Preheat oven according to the Instructions on the box.
- In a medium bowl mix together the brownie mix, Coke Zero and 2 egg whites. I used a whisk to really break up the brownie mix.

- Spray the donut pan with nonstick cooking spray. Pour half of the batter into a piping bag or zip lock bag. Add the batter to the donut pan. Mine does 6 donuts at a time.
- Cook donuts 16 minutes or until a toothpick is inserted into the donuts and comes out clean.
- Let donuts cool 5 minutes. Put powdered sugar into a mesh strainer and sprinkle over the donuts.
- Repeat steps 3-5 for the rest of the donuts.

Lunch
Kid-Friendly Baked Sweet and Sour Chicken
Prep+Cook time: 30 minutes, Servings: 8
5 Freestyle points per serving

Ingredients

- 2 pounds boneless skinless chicken breasts
- 1 Tablespoon olive oil
- 2 stalks green onion chopped
- 1/4 cup ketchup
- 1/4 cup honey
- 2 Tablespoons reduce-sodium soy sauce
- 2 teaspoons fresh ginger minced
- 1 Tablespoon garlic minced
- 1 teaspoon salt
- 1/3 cup rice vinegar
- 2 pouches Uncle Ben's Ready Rice whole grain

Instructions

- o Place the chicken breasts in a gallon-sized ziplock bag. Add all of the ingredients to the ziplock bag except the rice pouches. Close and mix to fully combine. Place in the refrigerator and let marinate up to 1 day, or as little as 30 minutes.
- o Preheat the oven to 425 degrees.
- o Once the oven is preheated, add the chicken breasts to a shallow baking pan (like a Pyrex dish). Pour the remaining marinade over the chicken (see note for an alternate method). Bake for about 20-25 minutes, or until the chicken is cooked through.
- o Remove the cooked chicken from the oven. Place on a cutting board and slice into thin slices. Microwave the 2 pouches of rice and serve immediately.

Nutrition info per serving : Calories: 197kcal, Carbohydrates: 11.7g, Protein: 26.1g, Fat: 4.7g, Saturated Fat: 0.9g, Cholesterol: 82.8mg, Sodium: 631mg, Fiber: 0.2g, Sugar: 10.4g

Dinner
Instant Pot Vegetable Noodle Soup

Prep 10 mins // Cook 11 mins Servings: 4
Points Values:4

Ingredients

- 1 onion, finely chopped
- 1 large carrot, diced
- 1/2 a small sweet potato - diced
- 1 clove of garlic, crushed
- 1/2 cup of frozen sweetcorn
- 1 tbs of tomato paste
- 1 tsp of paprika
- 1/4 tsp of garlic powder
- 1/4 tsp of chilli powder
- pinch of dried basil, oregano, thyme and parsley
- salt and black pepper
- 5 cups (1.2 litres) of vegetable or chicken stock
- 100g (3.5oz) of uncooked pasta of choice
- 4 handfuls of spinach
- spray oil

Instructions

- Set instant pot to saute mode
- Once hot, spray with spray oil, add onion, garlic and carrots and fry for 2 minutes to soften.
- Mix in the sweet potato, tomato paste and spices and herbs and stir to coat.
- Add the stock, sweetcorn and pasta, add lid, close valve and set to 8 mins high pressure.

- Once cooking is complete, do a quick pressure release and stir through the spinach. Season as needed with salt and black pepper.
- Optional: top with a little grated parmesan as part of your Healthy Extra A allowance.

Nutrition Facts Per Serving Amount Per Serving, Calories 171

DAY 22

Break Fast
Instant Pot Oatmeal

Prep Time 5 mins//Cook Time 5 mins Servings 4

Points Values:3

Ingredients

- 1 c oats use steel oats if you like a more turgid oatmeal
- 2 1/2 c water & 1 c apple skinned and diced
- 2 tbsp brown sugar & 3 tbsp butter
- pinch cinnamon , raisins optional

Instructions

- Put Instant Pot or pressure cooker on manual high pressure.
- Add butter and allow to melt. Turn Instant Pot off...important step to avoid "burn" message from showing up.
- Add water, oats, brown sugar, apples, cinnamon and raisins if desired. Stir
- Put lid on and close steam valve, set to manual high pressure for 5 minutes, do a quick release, open and serve.

Nutrition Facts Per Serving Amount Per Serving (6 oz) /Calories 192 Calories from Fat 90/ Total Fat 10g 15% / Saturated Fat 5g 25% /Cholesterol 22mg 7%

Lunch
5 Instant Pot Chicken Cacciatore

Total Time:35 mins, Servings : 4, Serving Size: 1 thigh with 1/2 cup sauce, **Points Values: 3**

Ingredients:
- 4 chicken thighs, with the bone, skin removed
- kosher salt and fresh pepper to taste
- olive oil spray
- 1/2 can (14 oz) crushed tomatoes (Tuttorosso my favorite!)
- 1/2 cup diced onion , 1/4 cup diced red bell pepper
- 1/2 cup diced green bell pepper
- 1/2 teaspoon dried oregano , 1 bay leaf
- 2 tablespoons chopped basil or parsley for topping

Instructions:
- Season chicken with salt and pepper on both side.
- Press saute on the Instant Pot, lightly spray with oil and brown chicken on both sides a few minutes. Set aside.
- Spray with a little more oil and add onions and peppers. Sauté until soften and golden, 5 minutes.
- Pour tomatoes over the chicken and vegetables, add oregano, bay leaf, salt, and pepper, give it a quick stir and cover.
- Cook high pressure 25 minutes; natural release.
- Remove bay leaf, garnish with parsley and serve over pasta, squasta or whatever you wish!

Nutrition Facts Per Serving Calories: 133 calories / Total Fat: 3g / Saturated Fat: 0.5g / Cholesterol: 57mg

Dinner
Vegan Instant Pot Mushroom Soup

Prep Time 15 mins// Cook Time 25 minsServes : 4
Points Values:3

Ingredients

- o 2 tsp olive oil
- o 1 medium onion, chopped
- o 1 large celery stalk, chopped
- o 1 large carrot, peeled & chopped
- o 4 garlic cloves, minced
- o 8 oz. crimini mushrooms, sliced
- o 8 oz. shiitake mushrooms, stems removed, sliced
- o 1 tsp dried thyme
- o 1/2 tsp ground pepper
- o 3 cups high-quality vegetable broth
- o 1/2 tsp kosher salt
- o 2/3 cup lite coconut milk

Instructions

- Set the Instant Pot to Saute mode. Heat the olive oil, then add the onion, celery and carrots. Saute the vegetables, stirring occasionally, until starting to soften, 3 to 4 minutes.
- Add the garlic, crimini and shiitake mushrooms, thyme and pepper. Cook until the mushrooms are starting to release their liquid, 2 to 3 minutes. Stir in the broth and salt.
- Put the lid on the Instant Pot, close the steam vent and set to HIGH pressure using the manual setting. Decrease

the time to 10 minutes. It will take the Instant Pot about 10 minutes to reach pressure.

- Once the time is expired, carefully release the steam using the quick release valve.
- Transfer half of the soup to the blender, add the coconut milk, hold on the top and blend until almost smooth (leave a little bit of texture), stopping the blender and opening the lid occasionally to release the steam. Transfer the pureed soup to a pot or bowl. Repeat with the second half of the soup.
- If the soup needs to be reheated, return it to the Instant Pot and heat gently over the Saute mode. Serve.

Nutrition Facts Per Serving   Serving Size   1 1/2 cups // Amount Per Serving As Served / Calories 108.3cal // Calories from fat 45

DAY 23

Break Fast
Apple Cinnamon Muffins

Prep+Cook time: 23 mins, SmartPoints : 3, Serves: 18

Ingredients

- 1 Sugar-Free Cake Mix (white or yellow)
- 1½ cups Granny Smith apples, chopped (approximately 3 small apples in ¼" dices)
- ½ cup unsweetened applesauce
- 1 small ripe banana , 1 cup water
- 2 teaspoons ground cinnamon

Instructions

- o Preheat oven to 375 degrees.
- o Spray with nonstick spray or line full sized muffin tins.
- o In a large bowl, mash banana and mix well with applesauce.
- o Mix together dry cake mix and cinnamon in large bowl.
- o Pour mashed banana and applesauce mixture as well as water over dry mixture and lightly mix, but don't completely blend.
- o Add in apples, and mix well.
- o Pour approximately ¼ cup mixture into each muffin tin. This should make enough for 18 muffins.
- o Bake at 375 degrees for 18 minutes or until golden brown and cooked through.
- o These will be moist, but should not be liquid in the center.

Nutrition info per serving : Makes 18 Muffins (using full sized muffin tin, but not overfilled muffins) 2 PointsPlus per muffin

Lunch
White Bean and Collard Green Soup with Rice

Prep/Cook time: 1 hour 5 minutes, Servings: 12 , 2 Freestyle points per serving

Ingredients

For the Beans

- 1 cup dry white beans soaked overnight in water
- 1/2 medium onion chopped
- 1 Tablespoon garlic minced
- 2 bay leaves , 1 Tablespoon salt

For the Soup

- 1 spray olive oil spray
- 1/2 medium onion chopped
- 2 stalks celery chopped
- 2 medium carrots chopped
- 2 teaspoons garlic minced
- 1 Tablespoon smoked paprika
- 1/2 teaspoon red pepper flakes
- 4 cups low-sodium chicken stock
- 1 cup canned crushed tomatoes
- 15 oz diced tomatoes drained and rinsed
- 3 sprigs fresh thyme
- 1/2 bag collard greens washed and chopped
- 1 Tablespoon sherry vinegar
- 3 cups brown rice cooked

Instructions
Cook the Beans:

- o Drain the beans. Combine all the bean ingredients in a large sauce pan. Add water to cover the ingredients. Bring this to a simmer over medium-high heat. Once it starts to boil, lower the heat to a simmer and cook for 35-40 minutes. Allow the beans to cool. The drain the beans and remove the bay leaves.

Make the Soup:

- o In a large stock pot, heat the olive oil spray over medium-high heat. Add the onion, celery, carrots and salt, cooking for about 8 minutes or until the vegetables are tender. Add the garlic, red pepper flakes and smoked paprika and stir until a lovely aroma begins.
- o Stir in the beans, chicken stock, crushed tomatoes, diced tomatoes, thyme and bring to a boil. Reduce the heat to medium-low heat and simmer uncovered for about 10 minutes.
- o Add the collard greens and the sherry vinegar and continue to cook until the collard greens are wilted and soft. Taste and add more salt or pepper, if needed.
- o To serve, add 1/4 cup of cooked rice to a bowl. Top with 1 cup of the soup mixture. You can add grated Parmesan cheese to the soup as well. Serve immediately.

Nutrition info per serving : Calories: 212kcal, Carbohydrates: 42.6g, Protein: 6.1g, Fat: 2.4g, Saturated Fat: 0.5g, Fiber: 3.4g, Sugar: 2.9g

Dinner
Healthy Banana Cake

Prep time: 15 mins // Cook time: 35 mins Serves: 16
Points Values:6

Ingredients

o cup shortening (you can replace with butter or margarine, but points change)
o 1 cup Swerve granulated sweetener
o 2 eggs
o 1 cup mashed ripe bananas, usually 2-3 bananas
o 1 teaspoon vanilla extract
o 1½ cups all-purpose flour
o 1 teaspoon baking soda
o ¼ cup low-fat buttermilk
o Ingredients for Cream Cheese Frosting
o 2 SmartPoints per serving when divided by 16
o 4 ounces light cream cheese, softened
o ¼ cup butter, softened
o 2 teaspoons vanilla extract
o 1 cup Swerve confectioners sweetener

Instructions

• Preheat oven to 325 degrees (dark pan) or 350 degrees (glass pan).
• Spray cake pan/casserole with nonstick cooking spray and set aside
• With a mixer, cream shortening and Swerve sweetener together until fluffy (approximately 3 minutes).

- Add eggs, bananas, and vanilla extract to the mixture and beat well.
- In a small bowl, combine the all-purpose flour and baking soda mixing well.
- Add flour and buttermilk to the liquid mixture and beat until just combined.
- Pour into a prepared cake pan.
- Bake for 20-35 minutes depending on pan choice (dark pan for 25-35 minutes, glass pan for 20-30 minutes). Check with a toothpick in the center to see if done completely.
- Remove from the oven and allow to cool completely.
- If adding cream cheese frosting, follow directions below:
- Add cream cheese, butter, and vanilla to a mixer and beat well until smooth. Slowly mix in the Swerve confectioners sugar until combined. Increase the speed and whip until you have a frosting consistency you prefer. Usually 2-3 minutes. You may add a bit of water or more confectioners sugar as needed to get the texture you prefer.
- Place icing in a piping bag and pipe in small amounts onto each square of the cake prior to serving.

Nutrition Facts Per Serving Calories: 199 kcal, Carbohydrates: 22 g, Protein: 2.8 g

DAY 24

Break Fast
Instant Pot Macaroni and Cheese Recipe

Prep Time 5 mins// Cook Time 5 mins Servings 8
Points Values: 7

Ingredients
- 12 ounces whole wheat shell pasta
- 4 cups low-fat and low-sodium chicken stock
- 1 cup fat-free half and half
- 6 slices Velveeta Original cheese slices
- 1/4 cup Parmesan grated
- 1/4 cup Fat-Free Cheddar shredded
- 1 tablespoon margarine
- 1 teaspoon garlic powder
- 1 teaspoon black pepper
- 1 1/2 teaspoon salt

Instructions
- Pour pasta, half and half, and chicken stock into Instant Pot liner and stir.
- Place lid on Instant Pot and set to seal.
- Choose manual and set to 5 minutes.
- Allow to come to pressure, cook, and when complete NPR (natural pressure release) for 2 minutes. Release remaining pressure, and set to saute.
- Add in cheese slices, margarine, garlic powder, salt, and pepper and mix well. Stir consistently until completely melted.
- Turn off saute feature and taste. May add salt and pepper to taste.
- Serve

Nutrition Facts Per Serving Calories 243 Calories from Fat 45 / Total Fat 5g / Saturated Fat 1g / Cholesterol 8mg

Lunch

Burrito Bowl

Prep Time10 mins //Cook Time25 mins
Servings: 6, **Points Values: 3**

Ingredients

- 2 frozen chicken breasts
- 1/2 cups uncooked brown rice
- 1/2 C dry black beans (not soaked)
- 1 - 15 oz can diced tomatoes, no sugar added
- 2 tbsp. Minced garlic
- 2 tbsp. Cumin , 1 tbsp. Onion powder
- 2 tbsp. Chili powder , 1.5 cups chicken stock

Toppings for Burrito Bowls:

- Romaine lettuce (green)
- Cheddar cheese (blue) , Avocado (blue)
- Salsa or pico de gallo (fresh is green)

Instructions

- Combine all the ingredients in the Instant Pot. Lock the lid into place and seal the pressure valve.
- Using the manual mode cook on high pressure for 25 minutes. When done release by turning the pressure valve to open, be sure to use a long spoon or a silicone oven mitt to move the valve.
- Open the lid and remove the chicken to shred. I use my mixer to shred chicken–it's SO easy to do! Just make sure to stand right there and watch because the chicken goes from shredded to ground pretty quickly.

- Add the chicken back into the Instant Pot, stir well.
- Measure and place the romaine lettuce in your bowl. Top with 1/6 of the beans, rice, and shredded chicken. Measure out and sprinkle with cheese, salsa, and avocado if you'd like!

Nutrition Facts Per Serving Calories: 464kcal /Carbohydrates: 40g / Protein: 56.3g /Fat: 8.1g / Saturated Fat: 0.4g /Cholesterol: 143mg

Dinner
Instant Pot Chicken Enchilada Soup

Prep Time: 10 mins//Cook Time: 30 mins Servings : 6
Calories: 231 kcal, **Points Values:1**

Ingredients

- 1 lb chicken breasts (skinless, boneless)
- 1 tbsp avocado oil , 1 small onion (diced)
- 4 cloves of garlic minced , 3 cups fat free chicken broth
- 15 oz can diced fire roasted tomatoes
- 10 oz can red enchilada sauce
- 15 oz can black beans (drained and rinsed)
- 2 cups frozen corn , 1/2 cup cilantro (chopped)
- 1 tbsp canned chipotles in adobo sauce (chopped)
- 1 tbsp ground cumin , Salt and pepper to taste
- Juice of 1 lime

Instructions

- Set Instant Pot to saute. When hot, add in oil. Then add in onions and garlic, and saute until tender, about 2 minutes.

- Pour in the chicken broth, enchilada sauce, diced tomatoes, chipotle in adobo sauce, beans, corn, cumin, salt and pepper. Stir well.
- Add in chicken breasts, making sure chicken is fully covered with sauce. Cover and cook on high pressure for 20 minutes. Release quick or natural.
- Shred chicken with two forks, and stir in cilantro and lime juice. Taste and adjust seasonings as needed. Spoon into bowls. Garnish as desired and serve.

Nutrition Facts Per Serving Calories 231 Calories from Fat 31 / Total Fat 3.4g 5% /Saturated Fat 0.3g 2% /Cholesterol 44mg 15% /Sodium 442mg 18% / Potassium 749mg

DAY 25

Break Fast
Pecan pumpkin pinwheels

Prep+Cook time: 47 mins, Ssmart points : 2, Serves: 20

Ingredients
- 1 package Pillsbury reduced fat crescent rolls
- ½ cup pure pumpkin puree , 2 Tbsp honey
- 2 Tbsp chopped pecans , ¼ tsp sugar
- ¼ tsp cinnamon

Instructions
- Unroll your crescent dough and separate into two pieces (4 crescent rolls to each piece) pinch together any holes there might be.
- Spread ¼ cup pumpkin puree onto each piece of dough, top each with 1 Tbsp of honey (you may want to put in a small zip lock bag, cut of tip and drizzle, to spread evenly) top with 1 Tbsp chopped pecans on each piece.
- Roll up dough pieces (long way) and put in freezer for 30 minutes.
- After they come out of freezer preheat your oven to 375F and spray a large baking sheet with some cooking spray.
- Using a serrated knife cut each roll into 10 pieces, I find the best way to cut is slowly cut into your dough then once you have broken through push down quickly to finish your cut. Place pinwheels on cookies sheet, you may want to use a knife to help place them so they don't stick to whatever you cut them on.
- Mix your sugar and cinnamon together and sprinkle on top of pinwheels.

o   Bake in oven for approx 10-12 minutes until dough looks golden brown ..Serve warm.

Nutrition info per serving :   Calories 48,Fat 2g,Sat fat 0.6g,Carbs 7.4g,Fiber 0.3g,Sugars 3.1g,Protein 1g

Lunch
Easy Chicken Salad

Prep/Cook time: 15 minutes, Servings: 6 , 3 Freestyle points

Ingredients

- 2 packages pre-cooked chicken chopped into chunks
- 1 cup grapes quartered
- 1/2 small red onion finely chopped
- 1 stalk celery finely chopped
- 5.3oz container plain Greek yogurt
- 1 teaspoon garlic salt
- salt and pepper to taste
- 4 large whole wheat English muffins optional
- 1 cup baby spinach torn

Instructions

o   In a small bowl, combine the chicken, yogurt, grapes, celery and seasonings. Stir until fully combined.

o   Toast the 4 English muffins and add the chicken salad to each one.   Top with the baby spinach.   Serve immediately.

Nutrition info per serving : Calories: 267kcal, Carbohydrates: 24.2g, Protein: 17.1g, Fat: 11.7g, Saturated Fat: 3.6g, Cholesterol: 53.3mg, Sodium: 203.8mg, Fiber: 2.3g, Sugar: 6.2g

Dinner
Instant Pot Skinny Steak Soup

Prep Time: 5 mins //Cook Time: 20 mins Servings: 4
Points Values:3

Ingredients
o 1 lb Steak or stew meat, fat trimmed
o 1 Onion diced , 2 Carrots diced
o 2 Celery Stalk diced
o 4 sweet peppers diced (or 1 large bell pepper)
o 8 oz mushrooms cremini, button sliced thin
o 2 tbsp garlic powder , 2 tsp celtic sea salt
o 2 tsp oregano , 1 tsp thyme
o 1 bay leaf , 1 cup crushed tomatoes
o 2 cups beef stock , 2 cups water

Instructions
- Set Instant pot to saute (or heat a large stock pot to medium).
- Add stew meat and brown.
- Add onion, celery, pepper, carrots, and cook until softened.
- Add mushrooms, cook until soft.
- Add spices, salt, water, and stock and cover instant pot, setting to seal. (or cover with lid and set to low if cooking on stove.)
- Cook on soup setting for 15 minutes (if cooking on stovetop, cook on low for 1 hour).
- Release steam and serve hot.

Nutrition Facts Per Serving Calories 364 Calories from Fat 153 / Total Fat 17g / Saturated Fat 7g / Cholesterol 69mg / Sodium 431mg

DAY 26

Break Fast
Easiest Salsa Verde Chicken

Total Time:2 hours 10 minutes Servings : 6

Points Values:

Ingredients:

o 1 1/2 lbs raw skinless chicken tenders
o 1/4 tsp garlic powder , 1/8 tsp oregano
o 1/8 tsp ground cumin , salt to taste
o 16 oz roasted salsa verde (I used Archer Farms), check labels for Whole 30 compliance

Instructions:

- Season chicken with garlic powder, oregano, cumin and salt and place in the bottom of the Instant Pot.
- Cover with salsa verde, cover and cook HIGH pressure 20 minutes. Quick or natural release.
- Remove chicken, shred with 2 forks.

Nutrition Facts Per Serving: Serving Size: 1/2 cup // Calories: 145 calories/ Total Fat: 2g, Saturated Fat: g , Cholesterol: 0mg

Instant pot Stuffed Pepper Soup Recipe

Prep Time10 mins // Cook Time8 hrs
Servings: 8, **Points Values: 3**

Ingredients

o 1 lb extra lean ground turkey or beef
o 1 cup onion, chopped
o 14.5 oz. can diced tomatoes with roasted garlic and onions
o 15 oz. can tomato sauce
o 2 cups green and red peppers, chopped (I've added up to four peppers, and it's yummy!)
o 3 cups beef broth
o ½ teaspoon basil
o 1.5 packets of chili seasoning
o 1 cup cooked rice, brown or white

Instructions

- Brown ground beef with onion in a skillet over medium heat.
- Drain beef and onions and place in instant pot.
- Chop peppers, add to instant pot.
- Add tomatoes (including juice) and remaining ingredients, except rice – which should be added 1 hour before end of cooking.
- Cover and cook on low for 6-8 hours.
- Natural pressure release for 10 minutes.

Nutrition Facts Per Serving Calories: 247kcal, Carbohydrates: 32.5g, Protein: 15.7g, Fat: 5.2g, Saturated Fat: 1.5g, Cholesterol: 41mg, Sodium: 1015mg, Potassium: 475mg

Dinner

Instant Pot Beef and Barley Stew

Prep Time: 10 Min, Cook Time: 45 Min

Serving Size: 1.25-1.5 cups, **Points Values:7**

Ingredients

o   1.5 lbs lean beef stew meat , 2 tsp flour

o   2 tsp olive oil & 1 onion, diced

o   1 cup carrots, diced & 1 cup celery, diced

o   2 tbsp. tomato paste & 4 garlic cloves, diced

o   6 cups beef broth & 2 bay leaves

o   3/4 tsp thyme & 2/3 cup pearl barley, rinsed

o   2 cups hash brown potatoes

Instructions

- Turn the Instant Pot on Saute mode. Once hot add the oil. Toss the beef with flour, salt, and pepper. Add to the instant pot and brown on both sides, about 5-7 minutes. You may want to do this in two batches to get a more intense flavor since the beef will brown more. Remove the beef and set aside.

- Add the onions, celery, and carrots. Cook for 4-5 minutes. Add the tomato paste and garlic. Cook until fragrant, about 1 minute.

- Add the beef broth, bay leaves, thyme, and pearl barley. Stir together.

- Close the Instant Pot and press the Soup/Stew button and set for 25 minutes. Let pressure release naturally once finished cooking. Open and add the potatoes. Let cook for 5 minutes until potatoes warm up. Season with salt and pepper.

- Slow Cooker Option: Follow steps 1 and 2 using a large pan. Add those ingredients to the slow cooker along with the broth, bay leaves, thyme, and barley. Cook on low for 8 hours. Stir in the potatoes and let cook for 10 minutes more or until potatoes are warmed through. Season with salt and pepper.

Nutrition Facts Per Serving Calories 329 //Calories from Fat 70

DAY 27

Break Fast
Air Fryer Monkey Bread

Prep+Cook time: 14 minutes, Smart Points : 3

Ingredients

- 1 cup self rising flour , 1 cup non-fat greek yogurt
- 1 teaspoon of sugar , 1/2 teaspoon cinnamon

Instructions

-
- In a bowl, mix yogurt and self rising flour. It'll appear crumbly at first, but keep going and the dough will form.
- Make a round ball of dough out of it. Then cut into 4ths.
- Take a wedge of dough and form a flattened circular disc (as shown in previous photo). Cut into 8 pieces (like a pizza). Take each wedge and roll into balls.
- Add cinnamon and sugar into a plastic ziploc bag, and then add your balls of dough. Seal the bag and shake well to evenly coat them.
- Light spray a mini loaf pan with non-stick spray. Add your dough balls, and sprinkle just a little bit of the cinnamon sugar mix on top. i used just a pinch as there was still a lot left in the bag unused.
- Place mini loaf pan in air fryer and bake for 7 minutes at 375 degrees F.
- Allow to cool for a couple of minutes and enjoy!

Lunch
Instant Pot Chipotle Chicken Tacos

Prep/Cook time: 35 minutes, Servings: 12, 4 Freestyle points

Ingredients

- 1 medium onion chopped
- 1 Tablespoon garlic minced
- 1 pound boneless chicken breasts
- 1/2 cup chicken broth
- 2 Tablespoons chipotle chiles diced
- 1 teaspoon brown sugar
- 1/2 teaspoon garlic powder
- 1 Tablespoon fresh cilantro chopped
- 1/2 small lime juiced
- lettuce , 1 medium tomato chopped
- 12 6 inch tortillas , 1/2 cup cheese shredded
- olive oil spray

Instructions

o
o With the cooker's lid off, spray the olive oil spray and heat to "Saute" until the cooker has heated up. Add the onion and garlic and cook until the onion is translucent and the garlic is fragrant.
o Season the chicken breasts with salt and pepper and place in the Instant Pot and saute until browned. Add the chicken stock, chilies, brown sugar, cilantro and lime juice. Securely lock the pressure cooker's lid and set to "Manual". Cook at HIGH pressure for 8 minutes.

- Perform a quick release to release the pressure. Open the lid and remove the chicken breasts. Shred the chicken and set it back in the cooker.
- Scoop out 1/2 cup of the chicken mixture onto a tortilla. Add lettuce, tomato and cheese, if desired and serve immediately.

Nutrition info per serving : Calories: 148kcal, Carbohydrates: 13.1g, Protein: 10.9g, Fat: 5.9g, Saturated Fat: 2.1g, Cholesterol: 29.3mg, Sodium: 108.3mg, Fiber: 1.9g, Sugar: 1.4g

Dinner
Beef and Tomato Stew
Prep Time: 20 Min // Cook Time: 23 Min
Serves: 8, **Points Values:6**

Ingredients

- 1 Tbsp olive oil (if searing the meat first)
- 2 lb. cubed stew beef
- 1 (15 oz) can stewed tomatoes
- 1 (6 oz) can tomato paste
- 2 cups beef broth
- 1 Tbsp Worcestershire sauce
- 1 medium onion, chopped
- 3 large carrots, sliced
- 3 ribs celery, chopped
- 1 cup fresh or frozen peas
- 1 lb. baby potatoes
- 1 tsp. salt & ½ tsp. pepper
- 2 tsp. garlic powder
- 1 Tbsp fresh thyme (or 1 tsp dried)
- 2 tsp fresh rosemary (or ½ tsp dried) & 1 bay leaf

Instructions

- To make in your instant pot: Drizzle olive oil in the bowl of your instant pot and turn on the sauté function. Wait until it's nice and heated then add meat, browning on all sides. Add the rest of your ingredients, seal the instant pot and select the meat/stew setting (about 35 minutes). Once cooking is complete, let the instant pot sit for about 12 minutes then release the steam by placing the valve to the venting position.
- To make in your slow cooker: Add cubed beef (except the oil) along with the rest of ingredients, cover and cook on low for 7 to 8 hours.
- To make on your stove top: In a large dutch oven or pot on medium high heat, drizzle oil and sear meat on all sides. Add the rest of the ingredients and bring to a boil, then cover and simmer for about 2 to 3 hours, until meat is tender. Serve and enjoy!

Nutrition Facts Per Serving Serving Size: 1½ cups / Calories: 325 / Fat: 13.3 g

Made in the USA
Monee, IL
02 October 2023

43827776R00061